Let Us Break Bread Together

BOOKS BY KENNETH W. OSBECK

25 Most Treasured Gospel Hymn Stories

52 Bible Characters Dramatized:
Easy-to-Use Monologues for All Occasions

101 Hymn Stories:
The Inspiring True Stories Behind 101 Favorite Hymns

101 More Hymn Stories:
The Inspiring True Stories Behind 101 Favorite Hymns

Amazing Grace:
366 Inspiring Hymn Stories for Daily Devotions

Count Your Blessings:
A Closer Look at 30 Hymns of Gratitude

Devotional Warm-Ups for the Church Choir:
Preparing to Lead Others in Worship

Let Us Break Bread Together:
A Closer Look at 30 Hymns About Fellowship

The Ministry of Music:
A Complete Handbook for the Music Leader in the Local Church

Hymn Stories for Real Life

Let Us Break Bread Together

A CLOSER LOOK
AT 30 HYMNS
ABOUT FELLOWSHIP

KENNETH W. OSBECK

COMPILED AND EDITED BY JANYRE TROMP

FOREWORD BY SELAH

KREGEL
PUBLICATIONS

Let Us Break Bread Together: A Closer Look at 30 Hymns About Fellowship
© 2024 by The Estate of Kenneth Osbeck

Compiled from Kenneth W. Osbeck's previously published works: *Amazing Grace: 366 Inspiring Hymn Stories for Daily Devotions* (Kregel, 2010); *101 Hymn Stories: The Inspiring True Stories Behind 101 Favorite Hymns* (Kregel, 2012, 2023); *101 More Hymn Stories: The Inspiring True Stories Behind 101 Favorite Hymns* (Kregel, 2013).

Published by Kregel Publications, a division of Kregel Inc., 2450 Oak Industrial Dr. NE, Grand Rapids, MI 49505. www.kregel.com.

Kenneth W. Osbeck's originally published hymn stories did not include source citations. However, the industry upholds Osbeck's works as credible sources, often citing his books as a primary source of information. We have done due diligence to find sources when possible and to include citations. For all others, we trust they can be found in Osbeck's selected bibliography, which we have included in this work.

We are grateful to PDHymns.org and Hymnary.org for providing sheet music for some of the public domain hymns included in this book.

Cataloging-in-Publication Data is available from the Library of Congress.

ISBN 978-0-8254-4252-0, print
ISBN 978-0-8254-6372-3, epub
ISBN 978-0-8254-6371-6, Kindle

Printed in the United States of America
24 25 26 27 28 29 30 31 32 33 / 5 4 3 2 1

CONTENTS

Contents

FOREWORD

WE HAD FIVE HOURS OF electricity every night where I grew up in Congo, Africa. When I was five, my parents decided to move back to the mission station founded by my grandfather Laban to start a Bible college and then a radio station. There were no paved roads, hospitals, telephones, gas stations, or grocery stores. We were isolated. Our family became closer than ever. Eventually, another missionary family moved to the station, and on Sunday nights, my mom would sit at the piano, my dad would play the organ, and we would sing hymn after hymn. This is how I learned to love the hymns. Since then, I have recorded almost one hundred hymns in the past twenty-seven years as part of the music group Selah.

When I was a teenager, my dad shared stories from Kenneth Osbeck's *101 Hymn Stories*, *101 More Hymn Stories*, and *Amazing Grace*. Stories like the one about Horatio Spafford, who wrote "It Is Well with My Soul" after he lost four daughters in a shipwreck, stuck with me. The words "when sorrows like sea billows roll" had so much more meaning. "The Love of God" was my grandmother's favorite song, and Dad always shared that the words of the third verse were written by a man in a prison. My father had read Mr. Osbeck's retelling of how the words were found on the man's cell wall after he died—that in a moment of clarity the man wrote these beautiful words based on a Jewish poem written a thousand years ago. In Africa, music always brought my family closer together. It was like breathing. It was second nature.

Let Us Break Bread Together: A Closer Look at 30 Hymns About Fellowship reminds me of the sweet fellowship that my family and I experience at the house church we attend. Our church follows the BLESS rhythms:[1]

• Begin in prayer
• Listen
• Eat
• Share your story
• Serve

Begin in prayer—We start with prayer because prayer opens up our fellowship with God and with each other.

Listen—We listen to the passage of Scripture for that Sunday and share our understanding of the passage with each other. We encourage our teenagers and middle schoolers to share their insights because the Holy Spirit speaks through them also.

Eat—We share a meal after every service. Have you ever noticed how many times in the Gospels Jesus is sharing a meal as he teaches others? Meals are sacred and a way of inviting someone into your family.

Share your story—We share our own stories about what God has been doing over the past week and ways that we have been able to speak life into others. This encourages the body of believers in our church.

Serve—We find ways to serve, whether clearing debris from a neighbor's yard after a storm or going on a mission trip to East Asia. We also serve each other by praying when someone in our church family is going through a difficulty.

Each week in our text thread, one of us takes a day to lead the Scripture reading. This week, my verses were Matthew 9:35–37. Based on the Discovery Bible Study (DBS) method, I answer three questions regarding the passage: (1) What does it say about God? (2) What does it say about me, whether positive or negative? (3) How do I live this Scripture out this week?

I would encourage you to ask the same three questions as you read about these thirty hymns of fellowship. If you decide to lead a group in a study of this collection, I encourage you to use the BLESS rhythms and the three questions to create an environment where everyone gets involved. Start with prayer. Listen by reading the hymn's lyrics and the stories behind the hymns. Offer snacks and coffee, or ask everyone to bring something. Give people an opportunity to share how the hymn or story is speaking to them. We were created to be known and to know each other and our Creator. In practicing these rhythms, you will serve others and inspire them to do the same.

May your fellowship and relationships richly increase.

Todd Smith of Selah

INTRODUCTION FROM THE EDITOR

THERE IS A CORE OF who I am that is entangled in music. I grew up going to symphonies, singing in the church choir, and playing in some of the best bands and orchestras in the state. I was through and through a music-loving, clarinet-playing band geek.

Even now my house has a nearly constant musical score running underneath.

My husband is forever noodling on his guitars. I write to music and sing snippets of Broadway, Mother Goose, Louis Armstrong, *VeggieTales*, and hymns for my kids.

Music draws pictures and speaks words I cannot always form coherently . . . and I am a wordsmith by trade.

Perhaps that is why I vividly remember reading the original *101 Hymn Stories* when I was maybe ten years old. And it's these hymns and stories that gave me the firm foundation to walk through some of the most mired land imaginable—my parents' divorce, the death of my beloved grandfather, my own clinical depression, and the recliner next to my daughter's hospital bed while she fought for her life.

Looking back, I gratefully acknowledge it was the community of Christ, parading in with meals and encouragement, that gave me tangible evidence of God's love specifically for me.

And that is why I put together a book of Kenneth Osbeck's words about hymns that remind us of the power of the community of believers. In this book, you'll find updated readings from Osbeck along with a "Living the Melody" section intended to help you stand on the solid history of hymns when dealing with the mire of your own life.

Never forget, God is "able to do immeasurably more than all we ask or imagine, according to his power that is at work within us" (Ephesians 3:20). And part of that "more" is delivered through the hands, feet, and words of the faithful.

May you find God's beautiful community in your life today. And as a result of God's loving and powerful care, may you hold out your hands in offering to those around you.

Janyre Tromp

Let Us Break Bread Together

BLEST BE THE TIE THAT BINDS

DENNIS

John Fawcett, 1740-1817

Hans G. Naegeli, 1773-1836

1. Blest be the tie that binds Our hearts in Chris-tian love! The
2. Be - fore our Fa - ther's throne We pour our ar - dent prayers; Our
3. We share our mu - tual woes, Our mu - tual bur - dens bear; And
4. When we a - sun - der part It gives us in - ward pain; But

fel - low- ship of kin - dred minds Is like to that a - bove.
fears, our hopes, our aims are one, Our com - forts and our cares.
oft - en for each oth - er flows The sym - pa- thiz - ing tear.
we shall still be joined in heart, And hope to meet a - gain.

— 1 —

BLEST BE THE TIE THAT BINDS

*Anyone who loves their brother and sister lives
in the light, and there is nothing in them to
make them stumble.*
—1 John 2:10

AT THE AGE OF TWENTY-SIX, John Fawcett and his new bride, Mary, began their ministry at an impoverished Baptist church in northern England. After seven years of devoted service in meager circumstances, they received a call to the large and influential Carter's Lane Baptist Church in London. After the wagons were loaded for the move, the Fawcetts met their tearful parishioners for a final farewell.

"John, I cannot bear to leave. I know not how to go!"

"Nor can I either," said the saddened pastor. "We shall remain here with our people." The order was then given to unload the wagons.

"We just cannot break the ties of affection that bind us to you, dear friends." Mary Fawcett assured the little congregation of the bond of love she and her husband felt for their poor peasant parishioners. John Fawcett decided to express his feelings in a poem about the value of Christian fellowship.

The following Sunday, John Fawcett preached from Luke 12:15: "One's life does not consist in the abundance of the things he possesses" (NKJV). He closed his sermon by reading his new poem, "Brotherly Love."

John and Mary Fawcett carried on their faithful ministry in the little village of Wainsgate for a total of fifty-four years. Their salary was estimated to be never more than the equivalent of two hundred dollars a year, despite Fawcett's growing reputation as an outstanding evangelical preacher, scholar, and writer.

Among his noted writings was an essay, "Anger," which became a particular favorite of King George III. It is reported that the monarch promised Pastor Fawcett any benefit that could be conferred. But the offer was declined with this statement: "I have lived among my own people, enjoying their love; God has blessed my labors among them, and I need nothing which even a king could supply."

LIVING THE MELODY

Being in close relationship with others is not always an easy command to follow. As none of us is perfect, it often takes sacrifice and grace. But when community works as God intended, it is beautifully powerful and reflects God's love for us.

What Scripture Says

A new command I give you: Love one another. As I have loved you, so you must love one another. By this everyone will know that you are my disciples, if you love one another.
—John 13:34–35

Keep on loving one another as brothers and sisters.
—Hebrews 13:1

Wisdom from History

God hath not called him for himself alone
. . . but that he may bear fruit
Of souls, and many may through him be saved.[2]
—Saint Francis of Assisi (1181–1226)

Saint Francis was born to a wealthy Italian family but gave up his wealth in favor of seeking spiritual enlightenment. His search brought him to the feet of Jesus, where he dedicated his life to serving God through helping the poor and caring for the environment.

Application Questions

- Who are your Christian friends and fellow church members?
- What can you do to grow in your affection for other believers?
- How can you, as John Fawcett did, show a loving concern for the needs of your community?

THE CHURCH'S ONE FOUNDATION

AURELIA

SAMUEL J. STONE, 1839-1900

SAMUEL S. WESLEY, 1810-1876

1. The Church's one foun - da - tion Is Je - sus Christ her Lord;
2. E - lect from ev - 'ry na - tion, Yet one o'er all the earth,
3. 'Mid toil and trib - u - la - tion And tu-mult of her war,
4. Yet she on earth hath un - ion With God the Three in One,

She is His new cre - a - tion By wa - ter and the Word:
Her char-ter of sal - va - tion One Lord, one faith, one birth;
She waits the con - sum - ma - tion Of peace for - ev - er - more;
And mys-tic sweet com - mun - ion With those whose rest is won:

From heav'n He came and sought her To be His ho - ly bride;
One ho - ly name she bless - es, Par - takes one ho - ly food,
Till with the vi - sion glo - rious Her long - ing eyes are blest,
O hap - py ones and ho - ly! Lord, give us grace that we,

With His own blood He bought her, And for her life He died.
And to one hope she press - es, With ev - 'ry grace en - dued.
And the great Church vic - to - rious Shall be the Church at rest.
Like them, the meek and low - ly, On high may dwell with Thee.

— 2 —

THE CHURCH'S ONE FOUNDATION

Christ is the head of the church, his body, of which he
is the Savior.
—Ephesians 5:23

"THE CHURCH'S ONE FOUNDATION" WAS written during an especially heated period of theological controversy in England in
1866. An attack on the historic accuracy of some of the Old Testament books threatened to destroy the great cardinal doctrines of
the Anglican church. As a strong supporter of historic faith, Pastor
Samuel J. Stone refused to compromise on doctrinal orthodoxy. To
combat the skeptical liberal scholarship, Stone wrote twelve hymn
texts based on the Apostles' Creed, an ancient list of essential Christian beliefs about God. This particular hymn refers to the ninth
article of the creed: "I believe in . . . the holy catholic [universal]
church, the communion of saints."

Stone's conviction was that the unity of the church must rest solely
on the recognition of the lordship of Christ as its Head (Colossians
1:18) and not on the views and interpretations of men. His desire was
to write a hymn that would reaffirm Christ's lordship as the foundation of the church.

Described as the poor man's pastor, Samuel Stone demonstrated
his firm belief in the church as the instrument of Christ for meeting
the needs of people. Stone spent much time ministering to the poor
and underprivileged people in London's East End. It was said that
"he created a beautiful place of worship for the humble folk and
made it a center of light in dark places."

This is what the local church was meant to be—a spiritual hospital for hurting humanity, never an exclusive, private club for self-
righteous Christians. Called out from the world by God for himself,

the church consists of people who meet regularly for worship, inspiration, instruction, and fellowship. Then Christ our Head sends his own back into the world to represent him and to model his love for all mankind.

LIVING THE MELODY

Take a moment today to acknowledge and affirm the lordship of Christ. Tell God that you desire to live in unity with your fellow believers and to engage with the poor, widows and orphans, and the outcasts of society. Today look for one opportunity to be a light in a dark place.

What Scripture Says

Then he asked them, "But who do you say I am?"

Simon Peter answered, "You are the Messiah, the Son of the living God."

Jesus replied, "You are blessed, Simon son of John, because my Father in heaven has revealed this to you. You did not learn this from any human being. Now I say to you that you are Peter (which means 'rock'), and upon this rock I will build my church, and all the powers of hell will not conquer it.

—Matthew 16:15–18 NLT

Wisdom from History

Going to the people is the purest and best act in Christian tradition and revolutionary tradition and is the beginning of world brotherhood. Never to be severed from the people, to set out always from the point of view of serving the people, not serving the interests of a small group or oneself. . . . It is almost another way of saying that we must and will find Christ in each and every man, when we look on them as brothers.[3]

—Dorothy Day (1897–1980)

Day turned from atheistic to Christian belief while working as a journalist in New York City. She devoted her life to serving the poor and cofounded the Catholic Worker movement.

Application Questions

- Do you agree with Samuel Stone that our recognition of Christ's lordship is the foundation of living in unity with believers? How are the two connected?
- What is one way you will be a light in the darkness today?

HOLY, HOLY, HOLY

NICAEA

REGINALD HEBER, 1783-1826

JOHN B. DYKES, 1823-1876

1. Ho-ly, Ho-ly, Ho-ly, Lord God Al-might-y! Ear-ly in the
2. Ho-ly, Ho-ly, Ho-ly! All the saints a-dore Thee, Cast-ing down their
3. Ho-ly, Ho-ly, Ho-ly! Tho the dark-ness hide Thee, Tho the eye of
4. Ho-ly, Ho-ly, Ho-ly, Lord God Al-might-y! All Thy works shall

morn - ing our song shall rise to Thee; Ho-ly, Ho-ly, Ho-ly!
gold-en crowns a-round the glass-y sea; Cher-u-bim and ser-a-phim
sin-ful man Thy glo-ry may not see; On-ly Thou art ho-ly—
praise Thy name in earth and sky and sea; Ho-ly, Ho-ly, Ho-ly!

Mer-ci-ful and Might-y! God in Three Per-sons, bless-ed Trin-i-ty!
fall-ing down be-fore Thee, Which wert and art and ev-er-more shalt be.
there is none be-side Thee Per-fect in pow'r, in love and pur-i-ty.
Mer-ci-ful and Might-y! God in Three Per-sons, bless-ed Trin-i-ty!

– 3 –
HOLY, HOLY, HOLY

Oh come, let us worship and bow down;
Let us kneel before the LORD our Maker.
For He is our God,
And we are the people of His pasture,
And the sheep of His hand.
—Psalm 95:6–7 NKJV

"'HOLY, HOLY, HOLY, IS THE Lord God Almighty,' who was, and is, and is to come" (Revelation 4:8). These are the words of worship that the mighty cherubim proclaim day and night.

Worship is the cornerstone of a believer's spiritual life. It is only as a Christian truly worships that he or she grows spiritually. Learning to worship and praise God is a lifetime pursuit. We worship God not only for what he is doing in our personal lives but also for who he is—his being, character, and deeds.

"Holy, Holy, Holy" was written by Reginald Heber specifically for Trinity Sunday, a service that reaffirmed the doctrine of the triune Godhead—Father, Son, Holy Spirit.

Reginald Heber was born in the area of Cheshire, England, on April 21, 1783, to scholarly and well-to-do parents. At the age of seventeen he entered Oxford University, where his scholarship and literary abilities received much attention. Following his ordination to the ministry of the Anglican Church, he served for sixteen years at an obscure parish church in the little village of Hodnet in western England. Throughout his ministry he was known and respected as a man of rare refinement and noble Christian character. Heber was also noted as a prolific literary writer, making frequent contributions to magazines with his poetry, essays, and hymns.

In 1823 Heber was sent to India to serve as the bishop of Calcutta. This responsibility included not only India but the island of Ceylon and all of Australia as well. The pressures of this work, along with the humid climate of that area, wore heavily upon his health. One Sunday morning, after preaching to a large outdoor crowd of Indians on the evils of the caste system, he evidently suffered a sunstroke and died very suddenly at the age of forty-three.

One year after his untimely death, a collection of his fifty-seven choice hymns was published by his widow and many friends. Most of these hymns are still in use today.

LIVING THE MELODY

Spend some time today worshiping God for who he is. Marvel at his power and love. Then consider how you might gather with other saints to praise God together. If you're able, try bowing down in worship. Engage your imagination, removing your crown and laying it before him.

What Scripture Says

The four living creatures, each having six wings, were full of eyes around and within. And they do not rest day or night, saying:

"Holy, holy, holy,
Lord God Almighty,
Who was and is and is to come!"

Whenever the living creatures give glory and honor and thanks to Him who sits on the throne, who lives forever and ever, the twenty-four elders fall down before Him who sits on the throne and worship Him who lives forever and ever, and cast their crowns before the throne.

—Revelation 4:8–10 NKJV

Wisdom from History

The Church exists for nothing else but to draw men into Christ, to make them little Christs. If they are not doing that, all the cathedrals, clergy, missions, sermons, even the Bible itself, are simply a waste of time. God became Man for no other purpose. It is even doubtful, you know, whether the whole universe was created for any other purpose. It says in the Bible that the whole universe was made for Christ and that everything is to be gathered together in Him.[4]

—C. S. Lewis (1898–1963)

Lewis was a brilliant Oxford don who was skeptical of the Christian story. But he says that God unrelentingly pursued him until he could no longer believe in a world without God. Lewis spent the rest of his life as "Apostle to the Skeptics," as some have called him.

Application Questions

- What are three things that cause you to marvel at God? If you're struggling, look at the text from this hymn to get started.
- How might seeing God's creativity and beauty bring you closer to your fellow believers?

IN CHRIST THERE IS NO EAST OR WEST

ST. PETER

John Oxenham, 1852-1941

Alexander R. Reinagle, 1799-1877

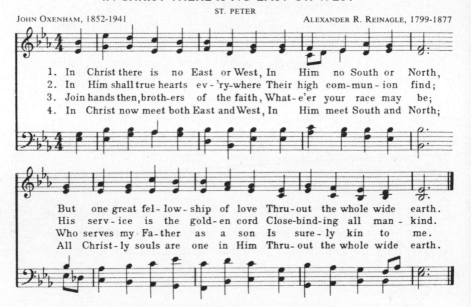

1. In Christ there is no East or West, In Him no South or North,
2. In Him shall true hearts ev-'ry-where Their high com-mun-ion find;
3. Join hands then, broth-ers of the faith, What-e'er your race may be;
4. In Christ now meet both East and West, In Him meet South and North;

But one great fel-low-ship of love Thru-out the whole wide earth.
His serv-ice is the gold-en cord Close-bind-ing all man-kind.
Who serves my Fa-ther as a son Is sure-ly kin to me.
All Christ-ly souls are one in Him Thru-out the whole wide earth.

Words from "Bees in Amber" by John Oxenham.

— 4 —
IN CHRIST THERE IS NO EAST OR WEST

*There is neither Jew nor Greek, there is neither slave
nor free, there is neither male nor female; for you are
all one in Christ Jesus.*
—Galatians 3:28 NKJV

WRITTEN IN 1908 BY THE noted English writer John Oxenham, this missionary hymn text was part of a script for a pageant at a giant missionary event, the Orient in London, sponsored by the London Missionary Society. It is estimated that over a quarter of a million people viewed the presentation from 1908 to 1914 both in England and in the United States.

An interesting account of the impact of this hymn relates an incident that occurred during the closing days of World War II. Two ships were anchored together, one containing citizens of Japan and the other American soldiers, all waiting to be repatriated. For an entire day they lined the rails, glaring at one another. Suddenly someone began to sing "In Christ There Is No East or West." Then another on the opposite ship joined in. Soon there was an extraordinary chorus of former enemies unitedly praising God with these words.

LIVING THE MELODY

Christ calls us to recognize not only that our differences make us stronger but also that they should be celebrated. We are to join hands with our brothers and sisters and be a people of peace. Visit a congregation in your area that worships differently from you. Notice the things that make Christ real in a new way. Or volunteer with an organization that helps with the homeless or orphaned, and notice how the needy contribute to society.

What Scripture Says

Then Peter replied, "I see very clearly that God shows no favoritism. In every nation he accepts those who fear him and do what is right."

—Acts 10:34–35 NLT

Above all, you must live as citizens of heaven, conducting yourselves in a manner worthy of the Good News about Christ. Then, whether I come and see you again or only hear about you, I will know that you are standing together with one spirit and one purpose, fighting together for the faith, which is the Good News.

—Philippians 1:27 NLT

Wisdom from History

Do not even give a single thought of separating from your brethren, whether their opinions agree with yours or not. Just because someone does not agree with everything you say does not mean that they are sinning. Nor is this or that opinion essential to the work of God. Be patient with those who disagree with you. Do not condemn those who do not see things just as you do, or who think it is their duty to contradict you, whether in a great thing or a small.[5]

—John Wesley (1703–1791)

Wesley was the son of a clergyman but felt something lacking in his soul. It wasn't until he was in his thirties that Christ became a real part of his life, and he embarked on a ministry to the commoners in the English countryside. Historians often cite his influence as preventing a bloody revolution.

Application Questions

- What is one way that the needy (orphans, widows, refugees, and others) contribute to society in general? To your community of believers?
- What can you do to celebrate a Christian tradition different from your own?

EVEN ME

Elizabeth Codner, 1824-1919

William B. Bradbury, 1816-1868

1. Lord, I hear of show'rs of bless-ing Thou art scat-t'ring full and free;
2. Pass me not, O ten-der Sav-ior! Let me love and cling to Thee;
3. Pass me not, O might-y Spir-it! Thou canst make the blind to see;
4. Love of God so pure and changeless, Blood of Christ so rich and free,
5. Pass me not! Thy lost one bring-ing, Bind my heart, O Lord, to Thee;

Show'rs the thirst-y land re-fresh-ing— Let some drops now fall on me.
I am long-ing for Thy fa-vor— Whilst Thou'rt call-ing, O call me.
Wit-ness-er of Je-sus' mer-it, Speak the word of pow'r to me.
Grace of God so strong and bound-less: Mag-ni-fy them all in me.
While the streams of life are spring-ing, Bless-ing oth-ers, O bless me.

REFRAIN

E - ven me, e - ven me, Let Thy bless-ing fall on me.

— 5 —

EVEN ME

May he be like rain falling on a mown field,
like showers watering the earth.
—Psalm 72:6

THE SPIRITUAL BLESSINGS OF A Spirit-filled life are intended for every believer, not just for a favored few.

The author of "Even Me" was Elizabeth Codner, the wife of a clergyman. She was having her personal devotions one day when she became deeply affected by a verse of Scripture, Ezekiel 34:26: "I will make them and the places all around My hill a blessing; and I will cause showers to come down in their season; there shall be showers of blessing" (NKJV).

Codner thought about the importance of water in the dry land of Palestine and related it to the necessity of the daily refreshment of the Holy Spirit and the Scriptures in a believer's life.

While she was still contemplating this truth, a group of young men from the parish called on her and shared the news of their recent trip to Ireland. Certain cities and areas of the Emerald Isle had experienced a spiritual awakening during the time of their visit. The young people were thrilled to have been witnesses of this event.

As they were describing their experience, Codner began to pray that these young men would not be content merely to have been spectators of the Holy Spirit's ministry but would also desire a genuine outpouring of his power in their individual lives.

With the words of Ezekiel 34:26 in mind, she challenged them with the remark, "While the Lord is pouring out such showers of blessing upon others, pray that some drops will fall on you."

The following Sunday morning, Codner stayed home from church because of illness, and with the impact of the young people's experience still fresh in her mind, she penned the challenging words of this hymn.

LIVING THE MELODY

Think about other believers whom you respect—it could be your pastor, a parent, a friend, or even a person you've read about. In what ways do their lives show the Holy Spirit's presence and power? Ask God in faith to give you a double portion of his Spirit (2 Kings 2:9).

What Scripture Says

"I will make them and the places surrounding my hill a blessing. I will send down showers in season; there will be showers of blessing. The trees will yield their fruit and the ground will yield its crops; the people will be secure in their land. They will know that I am the LORD, when I break the bars of their yoke and rescue them from the hands of those who enslaved them."

—Ezekiel 34:26–27

Wisdom from History

When [the true Christian] reflects on what Christ has done for him, he will groan for his own revival. When he hears someone tell a story about a fellow believer who is experiencing great joy in the Lord, he will groan for his own revival. . . . And may you turn your groanings into prayers. . . .

Begin, then, by humbling yourself—giving up all hope of reviving yourself, but beginning at once with firm prayer and earnest supplication to God: "O LORD, what I cannot, you do for me. O LORD, revive thy work!"[6]

—Charles Spurgeon (1834–1892)

Spurgeon was a fiery, imaginative preacher. He had a sharp sense of humor and shrewd common sense that made him popular enough that the Metropolitan Tabernacle was built specifically to host the masses who came to hear him. But he was also a man of the people, founding a pastors' college, an orphanage, and an organization that brought good books and medical help door to door.

Application Questions
- Who are the people you look up to spiritually?
- What is one area where you would like to see God revive his work in you?
- What do you desire for God to do in you that you cannot do on your own? Take a moment to pray and ask him for this.

BRETHREN, WE HAVE MET TO WORSHIP

HOLY MANNA 8s, 7s

1. Breth - ren, we have met to wor - ship And a - dore the Lord our God;
2. Breth - ren, see poor sin - ners round you Slum-b'ring on the brink of woe;
3. Sis - ters, will you join and help us? Mo - ses' sis - ter aid - ed him;

Will you pray with all your pow - er, While we try to preach the word?
Death is com - ing, hell is mov - ing, Can you bear to let them go?
Will you help the trem-bling mourn - ers Who are strug - gling hard with sin?

All is vain un - less the Spir - it Of the Ho - ly One comes down;
See our fa - thers and our moth - ers, And our chil - dren sink - ing down;
Tell them all a - bout the Sav - ior, Tell them that He will be found;

Breth - ren, pray, and ho - ly man - na Will be show - ered all a - round.
Breth - ren, pray, and ho - ly man - na Will be show - ered all a - round.
Sis - ters, pray, and ho - ly man - na Will be show - ered all a - round. A - men.

Words: George Atkins
Music: Traditional

— 6 —
BRETHREN, WE HAVE MET
TO WORSHIP

Finally then, brethren, we urge and exhort in the
Lord Jesus that you should abound more and more,
just as you received from us how you ought to walk
and to please God.
—1 Thessalonians 4:1 NKJV

THE APOSTLE PAUL'S FAVORITE NAME for fellow believers was *brethren*. He used this term at least sixty times throughout his various epistles. Paul's concept of the local church was a worshiping family—the family of God. While we need to worship God daily in our individual devotional lives, every believer also needs the enriching experience of worshiping and serving God with others on a regular basis. A church of faithful worshiping members is prepared to do God's work and fulfill its witness in the world.

While not much is known about George Atkins, the author of "Brethren, We Have Met to Worship," the hymn has been a favorite since it appeared in 1825. It remains a powerful appeal to the people of God to come together in prayer and worship.

Our worship of God, both personally and corporately, should share these five elements depicted in Isaiah 6:

- Recognition: "I saw the Lord" (v. 1).
- Praise: "Holy, holy, holy" (v. 3).
- Confession: "Woe to me!" (v. 5).
- Assurance of pardon: "Your guilt is taken away" (v. 7).
- Dedication: "Here am I" (v. 8).

LIVING THE MELODY

As believers, coming together in worship of our God is vitally important. There is a particular power in corporate learning and prayer that gives us sustaining strength. In the United States, Christians have the opportunity and blessing to gather more frequently and in unlikely places. As you read through or sing the hymn, think about ways you can contribute to your gathering of believers.

What Scripture Says

Let us consider how we may spur one another on toward love and good deeds, not giving up meeting together, as some are in the habit of doing, but encouraging one another— and all the more as you see the Day approaching.

—Hebrews 10:24–25

Wisdom from History

Perhaps, we are called to worship because this is the only safe, humble, and creaturely way in which men can be led to acknowledge and receive the influence of an objective Reality. . . . Thus worship purifies, enlightens, and at last transforms, every life submitted to its influence. . . . Worship is therefore in the deepest sense creative and redemptive. Keeping us in constant remembrance of the Unchanging and the Holy, it cleanses us of subjectivism, releases us from "use and wont" and makes us realists. God's invitation to it and man's response, however limited, crude or mistaken this response may be, are the appointed means whereby we move towards our true destiny.[7]

—Evelyn Underhill (1875–1941)

Underhill was a respected mystic and was the first woman to be invited to lecture on theology at Oxford University. She's well-known for her poetry, fiction, and nonfiction, in which she blended scholarship and devotion, writing on topics of mysticism, prayer, and the spiritual life.

Application Questions
- What does worship mean to you?
- Do you regularly meet for worship with other believers? If so, how do you help or participate in your community? If not, what might you do to find a community of believers?

FOR ALL THE SAINTS

SINE NOMINE

William W. How, 1823-1897

Ralph Vaughan Williams, 1872-1958

Unison

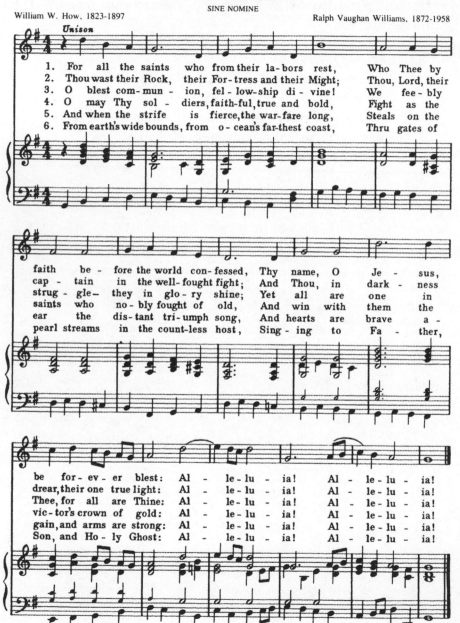

1. For all the saints who from their la-bors rest, Who Thee by
2. Thou wast their Rock, their For-tress and their Might; Thou, Lord, their
3. O blest com-mun - ion, fel - low-ship di - vine! We fee - bly
4. O may Thy sol - diers, faith-ful, true and bold, Fight as the
5. And when the strife is fierce, the war-fare long, Steals on the
6. From earth's wide bounds, from o - cean's far-thest coast, Thru gates of

faith be - fore the world con-fessed, Thy name, O Je - sus,
cap - tain in the well-fought fight; And Thou, in dark - ness
strug - gle — they in glo - ry shine; Yet all are one in
saints who no - bly fought of old, And win with them the
ear the dis-tant tri-umph song, And hearts are brave a -
pearl streams in the count-less host, Sing - ing to Fa - ther,

be for - ev - er blest: Al - le - lu - ia! Al - le - lu - ia!
drear, their one true light: Al - le - lu - ia! Al - le - lu - ia!
Thee, for all are Thine: Al - le - lu - ia! Al - le - lu - ia!
vic - tor's crown of gold: Al - le - lu - ia! Al - le - lu - ia!
gain, and arms are strong: Al - le - lu - ia! Al - le - lu - ia!
Son, and Ho - ly Ghost: Al - le - lu - ia! Al - le - lu - ia!

— 7 —

FOR ALL THE SAINTS

Therefore, since we are surrounded by such a great
cloud of witnesses, let us throw off everything that
hinders and the sin that so easily entangles. And let
us run with perseverance the race marked out for us.
—Hebrews 12:1

BISHOP WILLIAM W. HOW WROTE the text of "For All the Saints" in 1864 for use in the Anglican church liturgy for All Saints Day—the first Sunday in November and a day to give homage to departed saints. Here are some lessons the celebration of All Saints Day can teach us:

- Every believer whom God has called by his grace and sanctified by his Spirit has been called to sainthood.
- We should remember with gratitude those believers from our local church who were called to their heavenly home during the past year.
- We can thank God for that one particular individual who has especially influenced our lives—directing us to God, tutoring us in truth, and modeling the virtues of the Christian life.

Bishop How was affectionately known as "the people's bishop" throughout the city of London. His untiring energy and genuine interest in the spiritual welfare of the common people brought him respect and love from all who knew him. He once wrote a striking description of the characteristics he believed should be found in an ideal minister of the gospel—such as "pure, holy, . . . infinitely compassionate; of tenderest love to all; . . . wholly without thought of self." Those who knew him best said it was almost a perfect description of his own life and ministry.

When the beloved bishop died while vacationing in Ireland, he was greatly mourned by those he directly served as well as by the Christian church at large, who used his hymns, published sermons, poems, and essays.

How do we best honor the memory of loved ones and friends who have contributed to our lives? By rededicating our own life to God, obeying him implicitly, and reaching out to meet the needs of others.

LIVING THE MELODY

Stories of how others have overcome trials act as encouragement for the times when we are struggling. The good news is that there is no shortage of believers who have left us a legacy to follow. Consider reading a biography of a missionary or other Christian worker. Some great examples are Billy Graham, Amy Carmichael, George Müller, Elisabeth Elliot, and Brother Andrew. Breathe a prayer of thanks for their faithfulness, and then perhaps thank someone in your community who has been a good influence, mentor, or encouragement to you.

What Scripture Says

> In you our ancestors put their trust;
>> they trusted and you delivered them.
> To you they cried out and were saved;
>> in you they trusted and were not put to shame.
>> —Psalm 22:4–5

Wisdom from History

> Pay attention to what I tell you: whoever you may be, always have God before your eyes; whatever you do, do it according to the testimony of the holy Scriptures; in whatever place you

live, do not easily leave it. Keep these three precepts and you
will be saved.[8]

—Anthony the Great (251–356)

Anthony was a Christian monk from Egypt known as the "Father
of Monks." As one of the first to sojourn into the desert wilderness
alone, Anthony was quite famous, a status that was reinforced when
his biography, *The Life of Anthony,* was written and disseminated by
Athanasius of Alexandria.

Application Questions
- How would you describe what it means to be a saint?
- Think of one person in your life whose spiritual life you ad-
  mire. What is it about him or her that you appreciate?
- How might you become a little more like the person you ad-
  mire?

COME, YE DISCONSOLATE

CONSOLATOR

Thomas Moore, 1779-1852-alt.
Thomas Hastings, 1784-1872

Samuel Webbe, 1740-1816

1. Come, ye dis - con - so - late, wher - e'er ye lan - guish—
2. Joy of the des - o - late, light of the stray - ing,
3. Here see the Bread of Life, see wa - ters flow - ing

Come to the mer - cy-seat, fer-vent-ly kneel; Here bring your wounded hearts,
Hope of the pen - i - tent, fade-less and pure! Here speaks the Com-fort - er,
Forth from the throne of God, pure from a - bove; Come to the feast of love —

here tell your an - guish: Earth has no sor-row that heav'n can-not heal.
ten - der - ly say - ing, "Earth has no sor-row that heav'n can-not cure."
come ev - er know-ing Earth has no sor-row but heav'n can re - move.

— 8 —
COME, YE DISCONSOLATE

You will seek me and find me
when you seek me with all your heart.
—Jeremiah 29:13

He has sent Me to heal the brokenhearted,
To proclaim liberty to the captives
And recovery of sight to the blind,
To set at liberty those who are oppressed.
—Luke 4:18 NKJV

THE AUTHOR OF "COME, YE Disconsolate," Thomas Moore, was well known in Ireland for his poems and ballads, such as "The Last Rose of Summer" and "Believe Me, If All Those Endearing Young Charms." He became known as the "Voice of Ireland." Moore's prose and poetry were said to be influential in the political emancipation of Ireland. The English seemed to sense in his writings the true spirit of the Irish people, and they were moved to be more sympathetic toward the Irish desire for independence.

After Thomas Moore included "Come, Ye Disconsolate" in his 1824 collection, *Sacred Songs—Duets and Trios,* Thomas Hastings, an American hymnist, made a number of revisions in the lines. The third stanza was almost completely rewritten by Hastings. It is generally agreed that these changes made Moore's poem easier to sing and more suitable for church use.

With the repetition the plea to "come" and the plaintive promise that "earth has no sorrow that heav'n cannot heal," this hymn has brought divine peace and consolation to countless troubled individuals. The text assures the anguished, the desolate, the straying, and the penitent that responding to God's gracious invitation and sharing our burdens with him will bring us joy, light, hope, and tender comfort.

LIVING THE MELODY

Today bring to the mercy seat whatever is clouding your life. Lift up your heart's desire for Jesus to be near. Acknowledge that God delivers and heals. Perhaps God's comfort will come through a friend, a doctor, a neighbor, or even this hymn. Whatever the means may be, you will find the consolation and peace that God has promised and that only he can give. Then remember that the world is full of people with heavy hearts, and share a word of encouragement with someone.

What Scripture Says

Praise be to the God and Father of our Lord Jesus Christ, the Father of compassion and the God of all comfort, who comforts us in all our troubles, so that we can comfort those in any trouble with the comfort we ourselves receive from God. For just as we share abundantly in the sufferings of Christ, so also our comfort abounds through Christ. If we are distressed, it is for your comfort and salvation; if we are comforted, it is for your comfort, which produces in you patient endurance of the same sufferings we suffer. And our hope for you is firm, because we know that just as you share in our sufferings, so also you share in our comfort.

—2 Corinthians 1:3–7

Wisdom from History

When Jesus is near, all is well and nothing seems difficult. When He is absent, all is hard. When Jesus does not speak within, all other comfort is empty, but if He says only a word, it brings great consolation. . . . Be humble and peaceful, and Jesus will be with you. Be devout and calm, and He will remain with you.[9]

—Thomas à Kempis (ca. 1380–1471)

À Kempis was a German-Dutch priest who, early in his life, copied the Bible no fewer than four times. Later in life he was charged with instructing the novices, and much of his writing originates out of that period of his life.

Application Questions

- What area of your life could use the quiet touch of our Savior's love?
- With whom will you share a word of encouragement today?

COME, CHRISTIANS, JOIN TO SING

1. Come, Chris - tians, join to sing Al - le - lu - ia! A men!
2. Come, lift your hearts on high; Al - le - lu - ia! A - men!
3. Praise yet our Christ a - gain; Al - le - lu - ia! A - men!

Loud praise to Christ our King; Al - le - lu - ia! A men!
Let prais - es fill the sky; Al - le - lu - ia! A - men!
Life shall not end the strain; Al - le - lu - ia! A - men!

Let all, with heart and voice, Be - fore His throne re - joice;
He is our guide and friend; To us He'll con - de - scend;
On heav - en's bliss - ful shore His good - ness we'll a - dore,

Praise is His gra - cious choice: Al - le - lu - ia! A - men!
His love shall nev - er end: Al - le - lu - ia! A - men!
Sing - ing for - ev - er more, "Al - le - lu - ia! A - men!" A - men.

Words: Christian Henry Bateman
Music: "The Spanish Hymn"

— 9 —
COME, CHRISTIANS, JOIN TO SING

Come, let us sing for joy to the LORD;
let us shout aloud to the Rock of our salvation.
Let us come before him with thanksgiving
and extol him with music and song.
—Psalm 95:1–2

ORIGINALLY TITLED "COME, CHILDREN, JOIN to Sing," this joyful hymn first appeared in the 1843 collection *Sacred Melodies for Sabbath Schools and Families*, edited by the hymn's author, Christian Henry Bateman. Bateman served three Congregational churches in Scotland and England and was then ordained in the Anglican church.

Christianity is a singing faith, for sacred song is the natural outpouring of joyous hearts. But singing need not be limited to the church services; rather, it can become part of the Christian's normal daily lifestyle.

Singing God's praises provides many important benefits to believers:

- We become aware that God is pleased when our voices are lifted in praise; those who offer praise honor God (Psalm 50:23).
- We learn important spiritual truths and concepts when we sing. For many of us, our first awareness that God loves us and that he loves all the children of the world was gained through a song learned at our mother's knee or in the Sunday school nursery.
- Singing provides encouragement and comfort in times of need. Often when we are experiencing periods of discouragement and despondency, a simple hymn will come to mind and will be used of God to mend our fragile emotions.
- Singing is one of our best preparations for heaven. The Bible

LET US BREAK BREAD TOGETHER

teaches that we will enjoy giving praise and singing throughout eternity.

LIVING THE MELODY

Scripture doesn't promise us an easy life, but it does promise that we
will "see the goodness of the LORD in the land of the living" (Psalm
27:13). When tempted to complain or feel despondent, determine to
listen to or sing a song of praise. If you're in the company of others
and the environment is a stressful one, know that the gift of song
can be a powerful way to join with other believers. You can listen
together, sing together, or simply talk with others about songs that
fill you up. It is one of the best ways to experience calm and content-
ment.

What Scripture Says

> Be filled with the Spirit, speaking to one another with psalms,
> hymns, and songs from the Spirit. Sing and make music from
> your heart to the Lord.
>
> —Ephesians 5:18–19

> Let the message about Christ, in all its richness, fill your
> lives. Teach and counsel each other with all the wisdom he
> gives. Sing psalms and hymns and spiritual songs to God
> with thankful hearts.
>
> —Colossians 3:16 NLT

Wisdom from History

> Singing will set alight the Spirit. . . . The Apostle refers to
> spiritual rapture when he says, "Be filled with the Spirit"
> (Ephesians 5:18), and he shows us how to attain this, namely
> by "unceasingly singing praises to God, entering deeply into
> oneself and always stimulating thought." That is to say: by
> singing with the tongue and heart.[10]
>
> —Theophan the Recluse (1815–1894)

48

Theophan was a Russian Orthodox priest and the bishop of Tambov. He wrote many books that emphasized the importance of cultivating an interior life of continuous prayer.

Application Questions

- How might joining with fellow believers in song help in an area of your life where you're currently struggling?
- Where do you see the goodness of God in the land of the living?

ALL CREATURES OF OUR GOD AND KING

LASST UNS ERFREUEN

FRANCIS OF ASSISI, 1182-1226
Trans. by William H. Draper, 1855-1933

From *Geistliche Kirchengesäng*, 1623
Arr. by Norman Johnson, 1928-

1. All crea-tures of our God and King, Lift up your voice and with us
2. Thou rush-ing wind that art so strong, Ye clouds that sail in heav'n a -
3. Dear moth-er earth, who day by day Un - fold - est bless-ings on our
4. And all ye men of ten- der heart, For - giv- ing oth- ers, take your
5. Let all things their Cre - a - tor bless, And wor-ship Him in hum - ble -
Praise God, from whom all bless-ings flow, *Praise Him, all crea-tures here be -*

sing Al - le - lu - ia, Al - le - lu - ia! Thou burn- ing sun with gold- en
long, O praise Him! Al - le - lu - ia! Thou ris - ing morn, in praise re -
way, O praise Him! Al - le - lu - ia! The flow'rs and fruits that in thee
part, O sing ye! Al - le - lu - ia! Ye who long pain and sor- row
ness— O praise Him! Al - le - lu - ia! Praise, praise the Fa-ther, praise the
low, *Al - le - lu - ia, Al - le - lu - ia!* *Praise Him a - bove, ye heav'n-ly*

beam, Thou sil - ver moon with soft - er gleam: O praise Him,
joice, Ye lights of eve - ning, find a voice: O praise Him,
grow, Let them His glo - ry al - so show: O praise Him,
bear, Praise God and on Him cast your care: O praise Him,
Son, And praise the Spir - it, Three in One: O praise Him,
host, *Praise Fa - ther, Son and Ho - ly Ghost:* *Al - le- lu - ia,*

O praise Him! Al - le - lu - ia, Al - le - lu - ia! Al - le - lu - - - ia!
Al - le - lu - ia! Al - le - lu - ia, Al - le - lu - ia! Al - le - lu - - - ia!

– 10 –

ALL CREATURES OF OUR
GOD AND KING

All Your works shall praise You, O LORD,
And Your saints shall bless You.
They shall speak of the glory of Your kingdom,
And talk of Your power.
—Psalm 145:10–11 NKJV

BORN IN THE 1200S, GIOVANNI Bernardone, who was better known as Saint Francis of Assisi, demonstrated through his own life the tender, humble, and forgiving spirit and absolute trust in God that his hymn urges others to have. At the age of twenty-five, Bernardone left an indulgent life as a soldier, renounced his inherited wealth, and determined to live meagerly and imitate the selfless life of Christ. As a mystic medieval monk, he spent his lifetime as an itinerant evangelist, preaching to and helping the poor people of Italy.

A tribute was written of him, saying, "Saint Francis came to preach. With smiles he met the friendless, fed the poor, freed a trapped bird, led home a child. Although he spoke no word, his text—God's love—the town did not forget."

As a great lover of nature, Saint Francis saw the hand of God in all creation. The magnificent wonders of nature reveal the majesty of God and glorify him, and Saint Francis urged others to respond with expressions of praise and alleluia. Throughout his life he made much use of singing and strongly believed in the importance of church music. In all he wrote more than sixty hymns for this purpose, and "All Creatures of Our God and King" is one that has survived the passing of these several hundred years.

LIVING THE MELODY

Today look for God in creation. Take a walk if you're able, or flip through photographs of nature. See what a sophisticated world God fashioned, and then join with your community and nature to sing the praises of the God who made us all.

What Scripture Says

Ah, Sovereign LORD, you have made the heavens and the earth by your great power and outstretched arm. Nothing is too hard for you. . . . Great are your purposes and mighty are your deeds. Your eyes are open to the ways of all mankind; you reward each person according to their conduct and as their deeds deserve.

—Jeremiah 32:17, 19

For from him and through him and for him are all things. To him be the glory forever! Amen.

—Romans 11:36

Wisdom from History

Meditation is the activity of calling to mind, and thinking over, and dwelling on, and applying to oneself, the various things that one knows about the works and ways and purposes and promises of God. It is an activity of holy thought, consciously performed in the presence of God, under the eye of God, by the help of God, as a means of communion with God.[11]

—J. I. Packer (1926–2020)

Packer lived in England until he was called to Canada to teach at Regent College. His spiritual journey was transformed by Puritan thought, particularly the writings of John Owen, and Packer became a theologian and the well-known author of *Knowing God*.

Application Questions

- What is one area of nature that fascinates you? How might you communicate to others the truth of God's loving care as evidenced in that part of creation?
- How can you encourage others in your community to praise God by meditating on his works in nature?

DEAR LORD AND FATHER OF MANKIND

John Greenleaf Whittier, 1807-1892

Frederick C. Maker, 1844-1927

1. Dear Lord and Fa - ther of man - kind, For - give our fe - v'rish
2. In sim - ple trust like theirs who heard, Be - side the Syr - ian
3. O Sab - bath rest by Gal - i - lee! O calm of hills a -
4. Drop thy still dews of qui - et - ness Till all our striv - ings
5. Breathe thru the heats of our de - sire Thy cool - ness and thy

ways! Re - clothe us in our right - ful mind; In pur - er
sea, The gra - cious call - ing of the Lord, Let us, like
bove, Where Je - sus knelt to share with thee The si - lence
cease; Take from our souls the strain and stress, And let our
balm; Let sense be dumb, let flesh re - tire; Speak thru the

lives Thy serv - ice find, In deep - er rev - 'rence, praise.
them, with - out a word Rise up and fol - low Thee.
of e - ter - ni - ty, In - ter - pret - ed by love —
or - dered lives con - fess The beau - ty of Thy peace.
earth-quake, wind, and fire, O still small voice of calm!

— 11 —

DEAR LORD AND FATHER OF MANKIND

In repentance and rest is your salvation,
in quietness and trust is your strength.
—Isaiah 30:15

SO OFTEN IN OUR MODERN lives, we attack our problems with frantic and hurried activity, creating unnecessary stress for ourselves. We easily forget that our heavenly Father can assist us in meeting our daily challenges with serenity and calm assurance. We need the quiet confidence in God and the peaceful resting in his eternal love that are reflected in "Dear Lord and Father of Mankind" by John Greenleaf Whittier, America's beloved Quaker poet. Whittier's poetic lines remind us so clearly to listen carefully for God's still, small voice of calm in the midst of all life's turbulence.

Whittier lived a quiet, godly life in his speech, dress, and writings. It has been said that he "left upon our literature the stamp of genius and upon our religion the touch of sanity." Whittier wrote, "A good hymn is the best use to which poetry can be devoted, but I do not claim that I have succeeded in composing one."[12] Hymnal editors, however, have since made seventy-five hymns out of his poems.

John Greenleaf Whittier's life expressed the steadfast rest in his heavenly Father's love that these words suggest.

LIVING THE MELODY

Breathe this prayer as you begin your activities today:

Lord, grant to me a quiet mind,
   that trusting Thee, for Thou art kind,

> I may go on without a fear
>> for Thou, my Lord, art always near.

Decide now to allow God to guide you and give you peace in this hectic world. Evaluate your activities, bring them before the Lord, release those to which you are no longer called, and recommit yourself to do the rest from a place of peace.

What Scripture Says

> You will go out in joy
>> and be led forth in peace;
> the mountains and hills
>> will burst into song before you,
> and all the trees of the field
>> will clap their hands.
>> > —Isaiah 55:12

> If it is possible, as far as it depends on you, live at peace with everyone.
>> —Romans 12:18

Wisdom from History

> If when you are doing your acts of worship and you do them in humble-mindedness as one who is unworthy, they are acceptable to God. But should there arise in your heart some proud thought and you consent to it, or if the recollection occurs to you of somebody who is sleeping or inattentive and you pass judgment on that someone, know that your labor is in vain.[13]
>> —Arsenius the Great (350–455)

Arsenius was a desert hermit who, after beginning as an imperial tutor, joined the monastic community in Egypt. He then journeyed into the desert, pursuing a life of silence, contemplation, and humility.

Application Questions

- What is the purpose of rest? What is the purpose of godly activity?
- What can you do to refocus, eliminate, or recommit your activities so they align with God's desire that you have rest?
- How does resting in God's love affect your fellowship with other believers?

GOOD CHRISTIAN FRIENDS, REJOICE

1 Good Chris - tian friends, re - joice with heart and soul and voice;
2 Good Chris - tian friends, re - joice with heart and soul and voice;
3 Good Chris - tian friends, re - joice with heart and soul and voice;

give ye heed to what we say: Je - sus Christ was born to - day.
now ye hear of end - less bliss: Je - sus Christ was born for this!
now ye need not fear the grave: Je - sus Christ was born to save!

Ox and ass be - fore him bow, and he is in the man - ger now.
He has o - pened heav - en's door, and we are blest for - ev - er - more.
Calls you one and calls you all to gain his ev - er - last - ing hall.

Christ is born to - day! Christ is born to - day!
Christ was born for this! Christ was born for this!
Christ was born to save! Christ was born to save!

— 12 —
GOOD CHRISTIAN FRIENDS, REJOICE

Shout for joy, you heavens;
rejoice, you earth;
burst into song, you mountains!
For the LORD comforts his people
and will have compassion on his afflicted ones.
—Isaiah 49:13

AS THE SPRIGHTLY HYMN "GOOD Christian Friends, Rejoice" reminds us, Christmas is the most joyous season of the year for Christians. We have reason to be filled with gratitude to God for the immeasurable love shown to us in the gift of his Son. We can be exuberant in "heart and soul and voice!" This ancient hymn uses frequent repetition to impress upon us that the birth of Christ won for us "endless bliss" by opening the way to heaven and conquering our fear of death through his assurance of eternal life.

The festive spirit of Christmas, however, need not fade away as the holiday passes. The joy and peace that Christ brings to our lives enables us to be continually rejoicing Christians regardless of the circumstances. The blessings that came to us on Christmas morn will illuminate our lives forever!

"Good Christian Friends, Rejoice" is an unusual combination of fourteenth-century Latin phrases and vernacular German expressions. The original Latin text (1300s) was titled *In Dulci Jubilo*, meaning "in sweet shouting." Over the years German people added their own wording, making this a *macaronic* carol—one that combines two or more languages. The carol was later translated into English by John M. Neale, the noted nineteenth-century scholar and translator of ancient hymns. It first appeared in *Neale's Carols for Christmastide* in 1853.

LIVING THE MELODY

Look up some verses that contain the promises of God, write them on a three-by-five-inch card, and put the card where you can see it, or set the verses as the wallpaper on your phone or computer. Let it be a reminder of the joy of Christ's coming in your life. Actively look for an opportunity to build your community by sharing an encouraging word to someone who might be lonely.

What Scripture Says

> But the angel said to them, "Do not be afraid. I bring you good news that will cause great joy for all the people. Today in the town of David a Savior has been born to you; he is the Messiah, the Lord."
>
> —Luke 2:10–11

> Praise be to the God and Father of our Lord Jesus Christ, who has blessed us in the heavenly realms with every spiritual blessing in Christ.
>
> —Ephesians 1:3

Wisdom from History

> Oh, what love! Christ would not intrust [sic] our redemption to angels, to millions of angels; but he would come himself, and in person suffer; he would not give a low and a base price for us clay. He would buy us with a great ransom, so as he might over-buy us, and none could over-bid him.[14]
>
> —Samuel Rutherford (ca. 1600–1661)

Rutherford was a Scottish pastor, theologian, and author in the seventeenth century. He was prohibited from preaching and exiled to the town of Aberdeen, where he wrote many of the letters he is best known for.

Application Questions

- Which of God's promises are you most grateful for right now? Why?
- Is there a friend, coworker, or neighbor who might also need the encouragement of that promise? How might you share it with them today and grow in gratitude alongside them?

GOD LEADS US ALONG

1. In shad-y, green pas-tures, so rich and so sweet, God leads His dear
2. Some-times on the mount where the sun shines so bright, God leads His dear
3. Tho' sor-rows be-fall us and e-vils op-pose, God leads His dear

chil-dren a-long; Where the wa-ter's cool flow bathes the wea-ry one's feet,
chil-dren a-long; Some - times in the val-ley in dark-est of night,
chil-dren a-long; Thru grace we can con-quer, de-feat all our foes,

Chorus

God leads His dear chil-dren a-long. Some thru the wa-ters, some thru the flood,

Some thru the fire, but all thru the blood; Some thru great sor-row, but

God gives a song, In the night sea-son and all the day long.

Words and Music: G. A. Young

− 13 −

GOD LEADS US ALONG

You guide me with your counsel,
and afterward you will take me into glory.
Whom have I in heaven but you?
And earth has nothing I desire besides you.
—Psalm 73:24–25

THE AUTHOR AND COMPOSER OF "God Leads Us Along" was an obscure preacher and carpenter who spent a lifetime humbly serving God in small rural areas. Often the salary was meager and life was difficult for his family. Through it all, however, George A. Young and his wife never wavered in their loyalty and service to God.

After much struggle and effort, the Young family was finally able to move into their own small home, which they had built themselves. Their joy seemed complete. But then, while Young was away holding meetings in another area, hoodlums who disliked the preacher's gospel message set fire to the house, leaving nothing but a heap of ashes. It is thought that out of that tragic experience, George Young completed this hymn, which reaffirms so well the words of Job 35:10: "God my Maker, who gives songs in the night." The words of this hymn have since been a source of great comfort and encouragement to countless numbers of God's people as they experience the dark nights of their lives.

The more clearly we see the sovereignty of God and depend on his providential care, the less perplexed we will be by life's calamities.

He does not lead me year by year, nor even day by day;
But step by step my path unfolds; my Lord directs the way.
—Unknown

LIVING THE MELODY

Determine for this day and for this year to trust God more fully—regardless of the circumstances that may come your way. And as you walk with God, take a moment to notice others around you. Consider how they reach out to you and how you can reach out to them. Perhaps write a note or text to someone you know who is struggling. Ask how they're doing and how you can help. If you're the one who's struggling, reach out to someone in your community and ask them to step closer to you as you both follow God.

What Scripture Says

The LORD your God, who is going before you, will fight for you, as he did for you in Egypt, before your very eyes.
—Deuteronomy 1:30

When you pass through the waters,
    I will be with you;
and when you pass through the rivers,
    they will not sweep over you.
When you walk through the fire,
    you will not be burned;
    the flames will not set you ablaze.
—Isaiah 43:2

Wisdom from History

Our only desire and our one choice should be this: I want and I choose what better leads to God's deepening life in me.[15]
—Saint Ignatius of Loyola (1491–1556)

Saint Ignatius was a Spanish Catholic priest who helped establish the religious order of the Jesuits. He is highly regarded in the areas of prayer, mysticism, and decision-making, concepts covered in his book, *The Spiritual Exercises.*

Application Questions

- What is one area of your life where you struggle to trust God? How can you determine to trust God even while in the darkness?
- How might you reach out to members in your community to either help them or find help for yourself?

FAITH OF OUR FATHERS

ST. CATHERINE

FREDERICK W. FABER, 1814-1863

HENRI F. HEMY, 1818-1888
Adapted by James G. Walton, 1821-1905

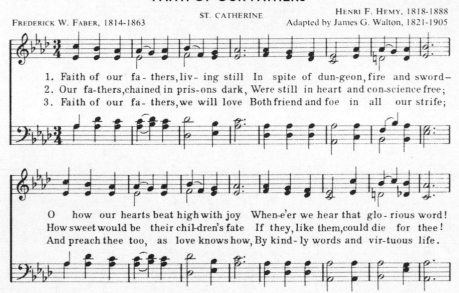

1. Faith of our fa- thers, liv- ing still In spite of dun-geon, fire and sword—
2. Our fa-thers, chained in pris-ons dark, Were still in heart and con-science free;
3. Faith of our fa- thers, we will love Both friend and foe in all our strife;

O how our hearts beat high with joy When-e'er we hear that glo- rious word!
How sweet would be their chil-dren's fate If they, like them, could die for thee!
And preach thee too, as love knows how, By kind- ly words and vir-tuous life.

— 14 —
FAITH OF OUR FATHERS

Contend for the faith that was once for all
entrusted to God's holy people.
—Jude v. 3

THE ELEVENTH CHAPTER OF HEBREWS has well been called the "great gallery of gallant Christian faith"—a thrilling account of spiritual giants who were willing to give all in defense of their faith in God. There have been martyrs of the Christian faith in every century since this New Testament record was first written. Even today, there are many who suffer and die because of their faith and profession of Christ as Savior and Lord. It is good for us to be reminded often that the history of Christianity is a rich heritage of myriads whose faith in God was considered more dear than life itself.

The "faith of our fathers" referred to in this hymn is the faith of the martyred leaders of the Roman Catholic church during the sixteenth century. Although he was raised as a Calvinist and later was a minister in the Anglican church, Frederick W. Faber—the author of this hymn—left the state church and joined the Roman Catholic fold, believing that a meaningful religious experience could be gained through liturgical church services.

Known as Father Wilfrid, Faber noticed the great lack of congregational hymnody that existed within the Roman Catholic church. He recalled the important and influential role that congregational singing had in Anglican churches, and he began to make it his life's mission to write hymns that promoted the history and teachings of the Catholic church. He wrote one hundred fifty such hymns before his early death at the age of forty-nine.

"Faith of Our Fathers" first appeared in 1849 in the author's collection, *Jesus and Mary; or Catholic Hymns for Singing and Reading.*

The three verses of this hymn challenge our commitment and loyalty to the gospel that our spiritual fathers often died to defend.

LIVING THE MELODY

Hebrews 11 lists some of the great biblical men and women and urges us to stand with them in faith. Read the chapter and ask God to make your Christian faith something that future generations will want to emulate.

What Scripture Says

> Our ancestors trusted in you,
>   and you rescued them.
> They cried out to you and were saved.
>   They trusted in you and were never disgraced.
> —Psalm 22:4–5 NLT

> I have fought the good fight, I have finished the race, and I have remained faithful.
> —2 Timothy 4:7 NLT

Wisdom from History

> It is good for him who knows his limitations to avoid the weight of being in charge of anything; but those who are firm in faith remain unmoved. If anyone wished to speak of the great saint Joseph he would have to say that he was not worldly. How greatly was he tempted and in that place where there had not yet been any trace of devotion towards God? But the God of his Fathers was with him and he delivered him out of all his trouble and now he is with his Fathers in the Kingdom of Heaven.[16]
> —Orsisius (n.d.–380)

Orsisius was a desert hermit and assisted in drafting the rules adopted by the communities of early monks.

Application Questions

- In what area of your spiritual journey are you strong? In what area are you weak?
- Do you sense God asking you to make changes in how you live out your faith? If so, in what ways?

NOT WHAT THESE HANDS HAVE DONE

AURORA

Horatius Bonar, 1808-1889

Norman Johnson, 1928-1983

1. Not what these hands have done Can save this guilt - y soul;
2. Not what I feel or do Can give me peace with God;
3. Thy work a - lone, O Christ, Can ease this weight of sin;
4. Thy love to me, O God— Not my poor love to Thee—
5. Thy grace a - lone, O God, To me can pard- don speak;
6. I bless the Christ of God, I rest on love di - vine;

Not what this toil - ing flesh has borne Can make my spir - it whole.
Not all my prayers and sighs and tears Can bear my aw - ful load.
Thy blood a - lone, O Lamb of God, Can give me peace with - in.
Can rid me of this dark un - rest And set my spir - it free.
Thy pow'r a - lone, O Son of God, Can this sore bond - age break.
And with un - fal - t'ring lip and heart I call this Sav - ior mine!

Tune: AURORA

— 15 —
NOT WHAT THESE HANDS HAVE DONE

Not by works of righteousness which we have done,
but according to His mercy He saved us, through
the washing of regeneration and renewing of the
Holy Spirit, whom He poured out on us abundantly
through Jesus Christ our Savior.
—Titus 3:5–6 NKJV

IN 1843, A REVOLT AGAINST the government-controlled church in Scotland began, and this disruption resulted in the separation of the evangelical party from the established church. The author of "Not What These Hands Have Done," Dr. Horatius Bonar, was one of the most respected and influential leaders of this revolt. He became known as an evangelical preacher of great renown as well as the most eminent of all Scottish hymn writers.

Bonar wrote several gospel songs for the famous Ira Sankey to use during crusade meetings in Great Britain. Other popular hymns by Horatius Bonar still in use in our hymnals today are "I Heard the Voice of Jesus Say" and the communion hymn "Here, O My Lord, I See Thee Face to Face."

"Not What These Hands Have Done" first appeared in Bonar's collection, *Hymns of Faith and Hope*, with the title "Salvation Through Christ Alone." It is a clear reflection of his strong Calvinistic theology that man's basis for God's favor and salvation rests solely on the finished work of Christ.

Bonar was highly respected throughout his life as a man of wide scholarship and culture. It was said that "his mind was saturated with the Scriptures." He loved children, and many of his hymns were written especially for them. His purpose for writing was "to fill my hymns with the love and light of Christ."[17] His remarkable ministry was characterized by earnest zeal, devotion, and a concern for soul winning. His many-faceted life was observed by some who said he was "always visiting," while others said he was "always preaching," "always writing," and "always praying."

LIVING THE MELODY

Honestly assess not only what you do for the kingdom of God but why you do it. As Bonar points out in this hymn, we often do good works to appease our guilt or to find peace or to make ourselves whole. Meditate on Christ's finished work and how you can "rest on love divine," finding grace, peace, and freedom.

What Scripture Says

> But he said to me, "My grace is sufficient for you, for my power is made perfect in weakness." Therefore I will boast all the more gladly about my weaknesses, so that Christ's power may rest on me. That is why, for Christ's sake, I delight in weaknesses, in insults, in hardships, in persecutions, in difficulties. For when I am weak, then I am strong.
>
> —2 Corinthians 12:9–10

Wisdom from History

> Sometimes when we read the words of those who have been more than conquerors, we feel almost despondent. "I feel that I shall never be like that," we feel. But they won through step by step, by little bits of wills, little denials of self, little inward victories, by faithfulness in very little things. They became what they are. No one sees these little hidden steps. They only see the accomplishment, but even so, those small steps were taken. There is no sudden triumph, no spiritual maturity. That is the work of the moment.[18]
>
> —Amy Carmichael (1867–1951)

Carmichael was an Irish missionary to India who, despite almost constant physical pain, opened an orphanage and founded an organization whose mission was partly to rescue temple children who'd been forced into slavery.

Application Questions

- When you look at the list of activities in your day, which ones do you do for the glory of God?
- Is God whispering about a change? Where might you start serving? Or where do you need to cut back so you can serve with a lighter heart?

JESUS CALLS US

GALILEE

Mrs. Cecil F. Alexander, 1818-1895

William H. Jude, 1851-1922

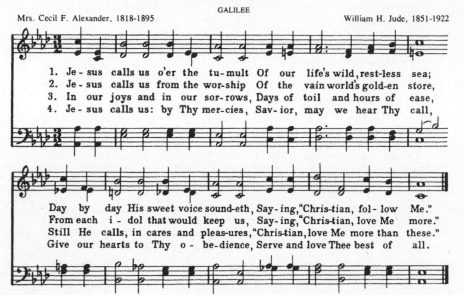

1. Je-sus calls us o'er the tu-mult Of our life's wild, rest-less sea;
2. Je-sus calls us from the wor-ship Of the vain world's gold-en store,
3. In our joys and in our sor-rows, Days of toil and hours of ease,
4. Je-sus calls us: by Thy mer-cies, Sav-ior, may we hear Thy call,

Day by day His sweet voice sound-eth, Say-ing, "Chris-tian, fol-low Me."
From each i - dol that would keep us, Say-ing, "Chris-tian, love Me more."
Still He calls, in cares and pleas-ures, "Chris-tian, love Me more than these."
Give our hearts to Thy o - be-dience, Serve and love Thee best of all.

— 16 —
JESUS CALLS US

Whoever serves me must follow me; and where I am,
my servant also will be. My Father will honor
the one who serves me.
—John 12:26

"JESUS CALLS US" WAS WRITTEN by Cecil Frances Alexander, who was recognized as one of England's finest women hymn writers. This hymn is one of the few by Alexander not specifically written for children. She believed that spiritual truths could best be taught through the use of songs, and nearly all of her more than four hundred poems and hymn texts were intended to reach children with the gospel.

Following her marriage in 1850 to the distinguished churchman Dr. William Alexander, who later became archbishop for Ireland, Alexander devoted her literary talents to helping her husband with his ministry, including writing poems he could use with his sermons.

One fall day, two years after their marriage, Dr. Alexander asked his wife if she could write a poem for a sermon he planned to preach for Saint Andrew's Day, a day commemorating the calling of Andrew by Jesus as recorded in Mark 1:16–18: "[Jesus] saw Simon and Andrew his brother casting a net into the sea; for they were fishermen. Then Jesus said to them, 'Follow Me, and I will make you become fishers of men.' They immediately left their nets and followed Him" (NKJV).

Dr. Alexander closed his sermon the next Sunday with the new poem written by his wife. The words of "Jesus Calls Us" have since been widely used in churches to challenge God's people to hear Christ's call as Andrew did and then to follow, serve, and love him "best of all."

LIVING THE MELODY

Andrew's quick response to Jesus is one we should endeavor to emulate. However, all of us have considerable "noise" in our lives—whether it's busyness or worry or apathy—that can prevent us from hearing God's call to serve him. Ask God to graciously provide fellow believers to help us hear and respond as Andrew did—to become one of Christ's faithful followers and "fishers of men."

What Scripture Says

I heard the voice of the Lord saying, "Whom shall I send? And who will go for us?"
And I said, "Here am I. Send me!"

—Isaiah 6:8

Then he said to them all: "Whoever wants to be my disciple must deny themselves and take up their cross daily and follow me. For whoever wants to save their life will lose it, but whoever loses their life for me will save it."

—Luke 9:23–24

Wisdom from History

Whatever weakens your reason, impairs the tenderness of your conscience, obscures your sense of God, or takes off your relish of spiritual things; in short, whatever increases the strength and authority of your body over your mind; that thing is sin to you, however innocent it may be in itself.[19]

—Susanna Wesley (1699–1742)

Wesley was the mother of nineteen children, only eight of whom survived her. Her life was not an easy one; it included poverty, a husband who was inconstant, and two house fires. But she was a spiritual constant in her community and in the lives of her children, two of whom became influential preachers—John and Charles Wesley.

Application Questions

- What things are in the way of your responding to God's call?
- Who are the people in your life who can help you increase your spiritual sensitivity to hearing God's voice?

LET US BREAK BREAD TOGETHER

1. Let us break bread to - geth - er on our knees,
2. Let us drink the cup to - geth - er on our knees,
3. Let us praise God to - geth - er on our knees,
   on our knees

Let us break bread to - geth - er on our knees;
Let us drink the cup to - geth - er on our knees;
Let us praise God to - geth - er on our knees;
   on our knees

Chorus

When I fall on my knees, With my face to the ris - ing

sun, O Lord, have mer - cy on me.
   on me.

Words and Music: Afro-American Spiritual

— 17 —
LET US BREAK BREAD TOGETHER

They devoted themselves to the apostles'
teaching and to fellowship, to the breaking
of bread and to prayer. . . .
All the believers were together and
had everything in common.
—Acts 2:42, 44

THE LOCAL CHURCH HAS BEEN described as a laboratory where believers learn to love one another regardless of color, nationality, or financial status. Our common heavenly citizenship is the one dominant tie that binds our hearts together.

One of the results of our weekly corporate worship is the growing bond of love and unity that develops between believers. This bond of fellowship can lead to God's family members learning to care for, honor, and serve one another in love, treating others with the same tenderness and understanding that we have experienced from God himself. Our determination to live in a love relationship with fellow believers is infinitely more important than the issues or differences that may separate us.

Christian unity does not mean that we must eliminate all diversities. We can differ with each other while maintaining love, respect, and a warm, unified spirit.

When our differences get out of hand and hard feelings develop, however, the communion service can always be a reminder that we must reconcile and once more restore a spirit of unity within the body of Christ. The bread and cup of the Lord's Supper should remind us of this truth each time we participate together (1 Corinthians 11:17–34).

LIVING THE MELODY

As a fellow child of the King of Kings, reflect on this statement: I should value those for whom Christ died and in whom Christ now lives.

The observance of communion offers us an opportunity to remember Christ's sacrifice for us personally, and we can also reflect on the truth that Christ has given his life for our brothers and sisters as well. Meditate on this and consider how you could promote more loving and caring relationships among the members of your local community of believers.

What Scripture Says

> How good and pleasant it is
> when God's people live together in unity!
> It is like precious oil poured on the head. . . .
> It is as if the dew of Hermon
> were falling on Mount Zion.
> For there the LORD bestows his blessing,
> even life forevermore.
> —Psalm 133:1–3

> May the God who gives endurance and encouragement give you the same attitude of mind toward each other that Christ Jesus had, so that with one mind and one voice you may glorify the God and Father of our Lord Jesus Christ.
> —Romans 15:5–6

Wisdom from History

> Unity in essentials, in non-essentials liberty, in all things charity.[20]
> —Rupertus Meldenius (1582–1651)

Rupertus Meldenius was the pseudonym used by Peter Meiderlin, a Lutheran theologian from Germany. He advocated for unity in the midst of disagreements between believers, publishing a book called *A Reminder for Peace at the Church of the Augsburg Confession of Theologians.*

Application Questions

- How does participating in communion help us to be more unified as believers?
- What is one thing you can do this week to promote love and unity within your church?

HAPPY THE HOME WHEN GOD IS THERE

1. Hap - py the home when God is there,
and love fills ev - ery breast; when one their wish, and
one their prayer, and one their heaven - ly rest.

2. Hap - py the home where Je - sus' name
is sweet to ev - ery ear; where chil - dren ear - ly
speak his fame, and pa - rents hold him dear.

3. Hap - py the home where prayer is heard,
and praise is wont to rise; where pa - rents love the
sa - cred Word, and all its wis - dom prize.

4. Lord, let us in our homes a - gree
this bles - sed peace to gain; u - nite our hearts in
love to thee, and love to all will reign

HAPPY THE HOME WHEN GOD IS THERE

As for me and my household,
we will serve the LORD.
—Joshua 24:15

My people will live in peaceful dwelling places,
in secure homes,
in undisturbed places of rest.
—Isaiah 32:18

THE HOME IS THE BASIC social institution of society, and the strength of any nation is in the quality of its homes.

Our homes are to be the holy of holies in our lives, places where ultimate love and acceptance are found between each individual. The real test of a parent's spirituality is his or her home life—the daily demonstration of a Christlike character.

For parents, the responsibility is not only to feed and clothe their children's bodies but to nurture their spirits, their minds, and their moral values. By word and by personal example, parents must carefully guide their children and fervently seek to show them what it means to be a Christian.

Good parenting also involves maintaining strong lines of communication between all members of the family. This demands quality time spent together in discussions, social times, daily spiritual retreats, and weekly periods of instruction and worship in the local church.

"Happy the Home When God Is There" was written by Henry Ware Jr., who later became a pastor in Boston, Massachusetts, and even mentored the American poet Ralph Waldo Emerson for a time. The hymn first appeared in *Selection of Hymns and Poetry for Use of Infant and Juvenile Schools and Families*, published in 1846.

LIVING THE MELODY

Whether your home is made up of children, grandchildren, roommates, or a community outside a physical dwelling, God can be the foundation of it. When God is in his rightful place, abundant love, joy, peace, patience, kindness, goodness, faithfulness, gentleness, and self-control can flow from our homes and bless our churches and communities. Ask God to grant you more of his Holy Spirit's power.

What Scripture Says

Direct your children onto the right path,
and when they are older, they will not leave it.
—Proverbs 22:6 NLT

Fathers, do not provoke your children to anger by the way you treat them. Rather, bring them up with the discipline and instruction that comes from the Lord.
—Ephesians 6:4 NLT

Wisdom from History

If we love our Creator, we trust in him alone. And love (the affection of charity, that is) produces only joy in the heart it possesses.[21]
—Saint Catherine of Siena (1347–1380)

Saint Catherine was a Doctor of the Church who worked diligently for its reform. She traveled widely and wrote extensively, pleading with those she encountered to repent and be renewed through total love for God.

Application Questions
- How would you define home? Where is your home?
- Is your home a place of abundance and love? If so, how are you bringing those Christlike attributes into the rest of the community? If not, how can you contribute to changing the atmosphere of your home?

LORD, I WANT TO BE A CHRISTIAN

1 Lord, I want to be a Chris-tian in my heart, in my heart.
2 Lord, I want to be more lov-ing in my heart, in my heart.
3 Lord, I want to be more ho-ly in my heart, in my heart.
4 Lord, I want to be like Je-sus in my heart, in my heart.

Bb(A)Cm(Bm)Ab(G)   Eb(D)   Ab/E(G/D)   Eb(D)

Lord, I want to be a Chris-tian in my heart.
Lord, I want to be more lov-ing in my heart.
Lord, I want to be more ho-ly in my heart.
Lord, I want to be like Je-sus in my heart.

Ab(G)   Eb(D)   Cm(Bm)

In my heart,   in my heart,
        in my heart,   in my heart,

Eb(D)   Bb7(A7) Cm(Bm) Ab(G)   Eb(D)

Lord, I want to be a Chris-tian in my heart.
Lord, I want to be more lov-ing in my heart.
Lord, I want to be more ho-ly in my heart.
Lord, I want to be like Je-sus in my heart.

— 19 —
LORD, I WANT TO BE A CHRISTIAN

He has given us his very great and precious promises,
so that through them you may participate in the
divine nature, having escaped the corruption in the
world caused by evil desires.
—2 Peter 1:4

"SIR, I WANT TO BE a Christian."

The text for this traditional spiritual, "Lord, I Want to Be a Christian," is thought to have been an outgrowth of this remark made by an African slave to a minister, William Davis, sometime during the mid-eighteenth century.

The word *Christian* was first used to describe the people of Antioch who believed the account of the gospel, personally accepting God's free gift of salvation and making Christ the Savior and Lord of their lives (Acts 11:26). They literally became *Christ*-ians—little Christs.

After taking the initial step of salvation, a Christian should develop a growing desire to model the virtues of godly living. The Bible teaches that Christians should make every effort to add to their faith goodness, knowledge, self-control, perseverance, godliness, mutual affection, and love (2 Peter 1:5–7). Christians, then, are to be effective representatives for God in a corrupt world and a living demonstration of the transforming power of the gospel.

A Christian is . . .
A mind through which Christ thinks;
A heart through which Christ loves;
A voice through which Christ speaks;
A hand through which Christ helps.
—Unknown

LIVING THE MELODY

Our culture tends to have a negative concept of what it means to be a Christian. This necessitates that we as a community be especially conscientious of how we conduct our everyday lives. Pray not only that you will be a worthy representative and demonstration of the gospel but that your church community will be as well.

What Scripture Says

Don't lie to each other, for you have stripped off your old sinful nature and all its wicked deeds. Put on your new nature, and be renewed as you learn to know your Creator and become like him.

—Colossians 3:9–10 NLT

Make every effort to add to your faith goodness; and to goodness, knowledge; and to knowledge, self-control; and to self-control, perseverance; and to perseverance, godliness; and to godliness, mutual affection; and to mutual affection, love. . . . Therefore, my brothers and sisters, make every effort to confirm your calling and election. For if you do these things, you will never stumble.

—2 Peter 1:5–7, 10

Wisdom from History

Are not all actions equal? Scripture says that Abraham was hospitable and God was with him. David was humble, and God was with him. Elias loved interior peace and God was with him. So, do whatever you see your soul desires according to God and guard your heart.[22]

—Nisterus (fourth and fifth centuries)

Nisterus lived in one of the three monastic centers in northern Egypt, Scetis (or Skete), now the Wadi El Natrun. He was sought out for his spiritual advice, and many of his sayings prove that he strove to be a "little Christ."

Application Questions

- How would you explain the term *Christian* if someone asked?
- How are you consciously trying to add Christlike virtues to your faith?

LOOK, YE SAINTS! THE SIGHT IS GLORIOUS

CORONAE

THOMAS KELLY, 1769-1854

WILLIAM H. MONK, 1823-1889

1. Look, ye saints! the sight is glo-rious: See the Man of Sor-rows now;
2. Crown the Sav-ior! an-gels, crown Him! Rich the tro-phies Je-sus brings;
3. Sin-ners in de-ri-sion crowned Him, Mock-ing thus the Sav-ior's claim;
4. Hark! those bursts of ac-cla-ma-tion! Hark! those loud tri-um-phant chords!

From the fight re-turned vic-to-rious, Ev-'ry knee to Him shall bow:
In the seat of pow'r en-throne Him, While the vault of heav-en rings:
Saints and an-gels crowd a-round Him, Own His ti-tle, praise His name:
Je-sus takes the high-est sta-tion— O what joy the sight af-fords!

Crown Him! crown Him! Crowns be-come the Vic-tor's brow.
Crown Him! crown Him! Crown the Sav-ior King of kings.
Crown Him! crown Him! Spread a-broad the Vic-tor's fame!
Crown Him! crown Him! King of kings and Lord of lords!

155

— 20 —
LOOK, YE SAINTS! THE SIGHT IS GLORIOUS

Great and marvelous are your deeds,
Lord God Almighty.
Just and true are your ways,
King of the nations. . . .
All nations will come
and worship before you,
for your righteous acts have been revealed.
—Revelation 15:3–4

THOMAS KELLY, AUTHOR OF THE text for "Look, Ye Saints! The Sight Is Glorious," was born in Dublin, Ireland, in 1769. He entered Trinity College with the purpose of studying law. While in school, he had a strong conversion experience and decided to study for the ministry. In 1792 he was ordained, eventually establishing a reputation as a magnetic preacher, warmhearted pastor, and excellent scholar. Kelly was especially respected and loved for his gracious, generous spirit, always giving liberally to those in need.

The text is considered one of the finest hymns celebrating Ascension Day, which occurs forty days after Easter and commemorates our Lord's ascent to heaven.

It is always thrilling to imagine the scene on Mount Olivet described in Acts 1. The Lord gave the disciples the parting blessing as well as his final instructions regarding their mission to be worldwide witnesses after being empowered by the Holy Spirit.

Then the One who had been nailed to a Roman cross just a short time before was dramatically taken up before their very eyes. And the two men dressed in white suddenly appeared and reminded the disciples that Christ's ascension must always be related to his return: "This same Jesus, who has been taken from you into heaven, will come back in the same way you have seen him go into heaven" (Acts 1:11).

LIVING THE MELODY

In a culture where it's easy to lose sight of the fact that Christ's kingdom is both coming and here now, let us remember that Christ is already crowned king. Rejoice in the truth that your Lord rose triumphantly and ascended into heaven victoriously to be your personal representative before the Father. And let us not forget the mission he sends us on, to "make disciples of all nations" (Matthew 28:19) while we await his return.

What Scripture Says

When they saw him, they worshiped him; but some doubted. Then Jesus came to them and said, "All authority in heaven and on earth has been given to me. Therefore go and make disciples of all nations, baptizing them in the name of the Father and of the Son and of the Holy Spirit, and teaching them to obey everything I have commanded you. And surely I am with you always, to the very end of the age."

—Matthew 28:17–20

Wisdom from History

The sun penetrates crystal and makes it more dazzling. In the same way, the sanctifying Spirit indwells in souls and makes them more radiant. They become like so many power-houses beaming grace and love around them.[23]

—Saint Basil of Caesarea (330–379)

Saint Basil was a bishop in Asia Minor (modern-day Turkey) known for the way he cared for the poor and emphasized that all people are equal in the sight of God.

Application Questions

- Where do you see Christ in your life right now?
- How can you be part of Christ's kingdom today?
- How does the reality of Christ's second coming affect your relationships with believers and unbelievers?

O COME, ALL YE FAITHFUL

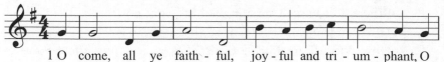

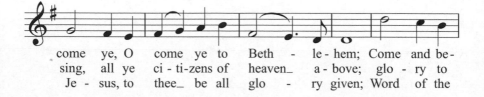

1 O come, all ye faith - ful, joy - ful and tri - um - phant, O
2   Sing, choirs of an - gels, sing in ex - ul - ta - tion,
3   Yea, Lord, we greet thee, born this hap-py mor - ning,

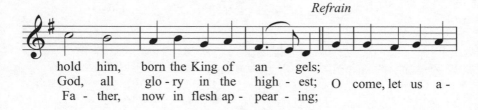

come ye, O come ye to Beth - le - hem; Come and be-
sing, all ye ci - ti-zens of heaven_ a - bove; glo - ry to
Je - sus, to thee_ be all glo - ry given; Word of the

Refrain

hold him, born the King of an - gels;
God, all glo - ry in the high - est; O come, let us a -
Fa - ther, now in flesh ap - pear - ing;

dore him, O come, let us a - dore him, O

come, let us a - dore him,_ Christ,_ the Lord.

— 21 —

O COME, ALL YE FAITHFUL

When the angels had left them and gone into
heaven, the shepherds said to one another, "Let's go
to Bethlehem and see this thing that has happened,
which the Lord has told us about."
—Luke 2:15

THE SONGS OF THE CHRISTMAS season are some of the finest musical compositions known to man, and "O Come, All Ye Faithful" is certainly a universal favorite. Today it is sung by church groups around the world, having been translated from its original Latin into more than one hundred other languages. The vivid imagery of the carol seems to have meaning and appeal for all ages in every culture.

The original Latin text consisted of four stanzas. The first calls us to visualize anew the infant Jesus in Bethlehem's stable. The second stanza is usually omitted in most hymnals, but it reminds us that the Christ child is very God Himself:

God of God and Light of Light, begotten,
Lo, He abhors not the Virgin's womb.
Very God, begotten, not created.
O come, let us adore Him . . .

The next stanza pictures for us the exalted song of the angelic choir heard by the lowly shepherds. Then the final verse offers praise and adoration to the Word, our Lord, who was with the Father from the beginning of time.

For many years this hymn was known as an anonymous Latin hymn. Recent research, however, has revealed manuscripts that indicate it was written in 1744 by an English layman named John Wade and set to music by him. The hymn first appeared in his collection *Cantus Diversi*, published in England in 1751. One hundred years later, the carol was translated into its present English form by an Anglican minister, Frederick Oakeley, who desired to use it for his congregation. The tune name, "Adeste Fideles," is taken from the first words of the original Latin text and literally means "be present, faithful."

LIVING THE MELODY

It's easy to lose sight of the miracles that Christmas celebrates and how they affect us. We serve a God who sent his Son to become a helpless human baby so he could not only save us but identify with us in our humanity. Let us, as the faithful, worship him and thank him for his sacrifice.

What Scripture Says

An angel of the Lord appeared to them, and the glory of the Lord shone around them, and they were terrified. But the angel said to them, "Do not be afraid. I bring you good news that will cause great joy for all the people. Today in the town of David a Savior has been born to you; he is the Messiah, the Lord. This will be a sign to you: You will find a baby wrapped in cloths and lying in a manger."

—Luke 2:9–12

The Word became flesh and made his dwelling among us. We have seen his glory, the glory of the one and only Son, who came from the Father, full of grace and truth.

—John 1:14

Wisdom from History

The Lord did not come to make a display. He came to heal and to teach suffering men. For one who wanted to make a display the thing would have been just to appear and dazzle the beholders. But for Him Who came to heal and to teach the way was not merely to dwell here, but to put Himself at the disposal of those who needed Him, and to be manifested according as they could bear it, not vitiating the value of the Divine appearing by exceeding their capacity to receive it.[24]

—Athanasius of Alexandria (ca. 296–373)

Athanasius was an early church father who was known for his struggles against certain emperors and heretical Christian sects. Today he is venerated as a saint and known by many as a pillar of the church due to his zealous support of Trinitarianism and the incarnation. He is called "the Father of Orthodoxy."

Application Questions

- What are some of your favorite memories of serving or worshiping with your community during the Christmas season?
- How can you show your adoration of Christ and what he's done?

SITTING AT THE FEET OF JESUS

1. Sit - ting at the feet of Je - sus, O, what words I hear Him say!
2. Sit - ting at the feet of Je - sus, Where can mor - tal be more blest?
3. Bless me, O my Sav-ior, bless me, As I'm wait - ing at Thy feet;

Hap - py place! so near, so pre - cious! May it find me there each day!
There I lay my sins and sor - rows, And when wea - ry, find sweet rest;
O look down in love up - on me, Let me see Thy face so sweet;

Sit - ting at the feet of Je - sus, I would look up - on the past;
Sit - ting at the feet of Je - sus, There I love to weep and pray;
Give me, Lord, the mind of Je - sus, Keep me ho - ly as He is;

For His love has been so gra - cious, It has won my heart at last.
While I from His full - ness gath - er Grace and com - fort ev - 'ry day.
May I prove I've been with Je - sus, Who is all my right - eous - ness.

Words: J. Lincoln Hall
Music: Anonymous

— 22 —

SITTING AT THE FEET OF JESUS

Mary has chosen what is better, and it will not be
taken away from her.
—Luke 10:42

THE STORY OF MARTHA THE worker and Mary the worshiper (Luke 10:38–42) illustrates an important spiritual principle: we please our Lord most when we learn to sit at his feet in adoration and worship *before* trying to serve him.

Sitting implies our humble dependence upon him and a sense of quietness of soul that indicates our willingness to hear. We can become so busy with life's pursuits, even worthy Christian activities, that we do not hear the still, small voice of God. Or sometimes we pursue God expecting only the spiritually spectacular. But like the story of Elijah on Mount Horeb (1 Kings 19:11–12), the Lord does not always reveal himself in the wind, earthquake, or fire, but sometimes in the stillness of the small voice.

> Speak, Lord, in the stillness while I wait on Thee;
> Hushed my heart to listen, in expectancy. . . .
> Speak, Thy servant heareth! Be not silent, Lord;
> Waits my soul upon Thee for the quickening word![25]
> —Emily May Grimes (1864–1927)

Learning to listen to God's voice is one of the important factors in our spiritual growth. When we are silent before him in the enjoyment of his presence and his Word, we gain his wisdom, his insights, and the renewal of our strength for daily living. May the people who see and know us say of us, as it was said of the early disciples, "these men had been with Jesus" (Acts 4:13).

LIVING THE MELODY

Take a moment to be still and assess whether you are living in humble dependence on God or working in your own strength. Be especially sensitive to God's still, small voice in your life. Let this awareness of his presence and concern encourage and empower you.

What Scripture Says

Because your heart was responsive and you humbled yourself before the LORD when you heard what I have spoken against this place and its people—that they would become a curse and be laid waste—and because you tore your robes and wept in my presence, I also have heard you, declares the LORD.

—2 Kings 22:19

I wait for the LORD, my whole being waits,
  and in his word I put my hope.

—Psalm 130:5

Take my yoke upon you and learn from me, for I am gentle and humble in heart, and you will find rest for your souls.

—Matthew 11:29

Wisdom from History

O Lord Jesus . . . it is so hard to be silent, silent with my mouth, but even more, silent with my heart. There is so much talking going on within me. It seems that I am always involved in inner debates with myself, my friends, my enemies. . . . If I were simply to rest at your feet and realize that I belong to you and you alone, I would easily stop arguing with all the real and imagined people around me. . . . I know that in the silence of my heart you will speak to me and show me your love.[26]

—Henri Nouwen (1932–1996)

Nouwen was a Catholic priest, professor, and writer from the Netherlands. He taught at Yale and Harvard but left academia to pastor a community of people with intellectual disabilities. He wrote extensively about learning to live as the beloved of God.

Application Questions

- Where do you sense you've been striving in your own strength?
- When might you set aside a time to sit at the feet of Jesus?
- How could you incorporate the practice of silence into your church community?

WE'VE A STORY TO TELL TO THE NATIONS

1. We've a sto - ry to tell to the na - tions That shall
2. We've a song to be sung to the na - tions, That shall
3. We've a mes - sage to give to the na - tions, That the
4. We've a Sav - ior to show to the na - tions, Who the

turn their hearts to the right, A sto - ry of truth and mer - cy,
lift their hearts to the Lord; A song that shall con - quer e - vil
Lord Who reign - eth a - bove Hath sent us His Son to save us,
path of sor - row has trod, That all of the world's great peo - ples

A sto - ry of peace and light, A sto - ry of peace and light.
And shat - ter the spear and sword, And shat - ter the spear and sword.
And show us that God is love, And show us that God is love.
Might come to the truth of God, Might come to the truth of God!

Chorus

For the dark - ness shall turn to dawn - ing, And the dawn-ing to noon-day bright,

Words: George Scriven
Music: C. C. Converse

PDHymns.com

— 23 —
WE'VE A STORY TO TELL
TO THE NATIONS

All nations will come and worship before you,
for your righteous acts have been revealed.
—Revelation 15:4

"A STORY TO TELL . . . A song to be sung . . . a message to give . . .
a Savior to show." This hymn is a concise summary of the task of
worldwide evangelization—we have a gospel that must be demonstrated as well as proclaimed.

The early Christians, though often fiercely persecuted by the Romans, successfully spread the news of Christ's death and resurrec-
tion. By AD 380, Christianity was recognized as the official religion
throughout the empire. Yet for the next one thousand years and
more, the flame of evangelism burned low.

The sixteenth-century Protestant Reformation saw a brief revival of fervor, but not until the eighteenth century did Christians
make their first serious attempt to organize missionary work. The
expansion of missions in the eighteenth and nineteenth centuries was
clearly connected with the waves of revival that were sweeping across
Europe and North America.

Since the close of World War II, the cause of world missions has
grown markedly. It is estimated that presently there are 445,000
missionaries serving.[27]

But the task is far from finished. More than forty percent of the
world's population is yet unreached with the good news of Christ.[28]
Nearly every mission board desperately needs more workers.

"We've a Story to Tell to the Nations," written and composed
by H. Ernest Nichol in 1896, is still widely sung by young and old

LET US BREAK BREAD TOGETHER

alike. It represents the missionary zeal that should always burn in our hearts.

LIVING THE MELODY

Take time to consider those who need to hear about Christ's "story of peace and light." Put a plan in place to reach out to those individuals. Become a part of their community, or welcome them into yours. And if God has spoken to you about stepping into a full-time missionary role, reach out today to a missions board where you might help.

What Scripture Says

He said to them, "Go into all the world and preach the gospel to all creation."

—Mark 16:15

Repentance for the forgiveness of sins will be preached in his name to all nations, beginning at Jerusalem.

—Luke 24:47

I have come into the world as a light, so that no one who believes in me should stay in darkness.

—John 12:46

Wisdom from History

It is clear from the New Testament that the Lord Jesus came as a Friend, *in order to help sinners to come to Him.* Our coming to Him was made possible by His first coming to us. . . . What the sinner cannot do the Savior is at hand to do for him. It is for this reason that we can tell people that they need not wait for anything, but can come to Him immediately. Whatever their state, whatever their problem, let them bring it and tell it to the Friend of Sinners.[29]

—Watchman Nee (1903–1972)

Nee was the head of the dynamic movement known as the "Little Flock." This group forged a Christian witness for indigenous Chinese people independent of foreign missions and governmental influence. Nee spent twenty years in prison, where he refused to betray Christ and continued telling others about God.

Application Questions

- Who can you reach out to with the love of Jesus today?
- How can you welcome that person into your community?

WE GATHER TOGETHER

KREMSER

Source Unknown
Trans. by Theodore Baker, 1851-1934

Netherlands Folk Melody, c. 1625
Arr. by Edward Kremser, 1838-1914

1. We gath-er to-geth-er to ask the Lord's bless-ing—He chas-tens and
2. Be-side us to guide us, our God with us join-ing, Or-dain-ing, main-
3. We all do ex-tol Thee, Thou lead-er tri-um-phant, And pray that Thou

has-tens His will to make known; The wick-ed op-press-ing now cease
tain-ing His king-dom di-vine; So from the be-gin-ning the fight
still our de-fend-er wilt be; Let Thy con-gre-ga-tion es-cape

from dis-tress-ing: Sing prais-es to His name— He for-gets not His own.
we were win-ning: Thou, Lord, wast at our side— all glo-ry be Thine.
trib-u-la-tion: Thy name be ev-er praised! O Lord, make us free!*

— 24 —
WE GATHER TOGETHER

Devote yourselves to prayer,
being watchful and thankful.
—Colossians 4:2

"WE GATHER TOGETHER" MUST BE understood and appreciated in its historical setting. For many years, the Netherlands had been under the scourge of Spain, and in 1576, the city of Antwerp was captured and sacked by the Spanish armies. Again in 1585, it was captured by the Spanish, and all the Protestant citizens were exiled.

Many other Dutch cities suffered similar fates. During the seventeenth century, however, there developed in the Netherlands a time of great prosperity and rich post-Reformation culture. Commerce expanded around the world, and this was also the period of great Dutch art, with such well-known painters as Rembrandt and Vermeer. In 1648 the Spanish endeavors to control the Netherlands were finally destroyed beyond recovery.

Freedom now belonged to the Dutch, both politically from Spain and religiously from the Catholic church. The text for "We Gather Together" was written by an anonymous author at the end of the seventeenth century to celebrate the Netherlands's freedom from its Spanish overlords, who had been driven from the land.

One can readily see the references to these historical events in the hymn's text: "The wicked oppressing now cease from distressing," as well as the prayer in the final stanza that God will continue to defend.

Today we often sing this hymn at Thanksgiving Day gatherings as an expression of thanks to God, our defender and guide throughout the previous year.

LIVING THE MELODY

For the Christian, thanksgiving must be a daily way of living. Consider making it a practice to write God a thank-you note every morning. Start your note with, "Lord, thank you for . . ." and then list three things for which you are thankful. Think about things like a miracle God has given you, some aspect of creation, a delicious meal, even a good conversation. Make it a practice to share with others how God has guided and protected you. You never know when someone might need the encouragement.

What Scripture Says

Let all who take refuge in you rejoice;
    let them sing joyful praises forever.
Spread your protection over them,
    that all who love your name may be filled with joy.
For you bless the godly, O LORD;
    you surround them with your shield of love.
                                        —Psalm 5:11–12 NLT

Wisdom from History

I arise today
Through the strength of heaven;
Light of sun,
Brilliance of moon,
Splendor of fire,
Speed of lightning,
Swiftness of the wind,
Depth of the sea,
Stability of earth,
Firmness of rock.[30]
    —Saint Patrick (fifth century)

Saint Patrick was forcibly taken from his home in Britain at the age of sixteen and transported to Ireland by pirates. He eventually escaped and returned home. But after becoming a cleric, he went back to the place of his captivity and became a missionary and bishop to the Irish.

Application Questions

- Look back at your life. What is a season that didn't go as you'd planned?
- How was God your defender and guide through that season?
- How can you encourage other believers with your testimony of God's goodness?

SOLDIERS OF CHRIST, ARISE

DIADEMATA S. M. D.

1. Sol - diers of Christ, a - rise, And put your ar - mor on,
2. Stand, then, in His great might, With all His strength en - dued;
3. Leave no un - guard - ed place, No weak - ness of the soul,

Strong in the strength which God sup - plies Thru His e - ter - nal Son.
And take, to arm you for the fight, The *pan - o - ply of God!
Take eve - ry vir - tue, eve - ry grace, And for - ti - fy the whole.

Strong in the Lord of Hosts, And in His might - y pow'r,
That, hav - ing all things done, And all your con - flicts past,
From strength to strength go on; Wres - tle, and fight, and pray;

Who in the strength of Je - sus trusts Is more than con - quer - or.
Ye may o'er - come thru Christ a - lone, And stand en - tire at last.
Tread all the pow'rs of dark - ness down, And win the well-fought day! A - men.

*(vs. 2) panoply: a full suit of armor

Words: Charles Wesley (1749)
Music: Sir George Job Elvey (1868)

− 25 −

SOLDIERS OF CHRIST, ARISE

Finally, be strong in the Lord and in his mighty power. Put on the full armor of God, so that you can take your stand against the devil's schemes.
—Ephesians 6:10–11

FOLLOWERS OF CHRIST ARE ALSO his soldiers, called to battle the forces of Satan and evil. Victories are never won while resting in the barracks. God's soldiers must always be alert and dressed in full armor.

That armor includes six important pieces (Ephesians 6:13–17):

- Belt of truth
- Breastplate of righteousness
- Sandals of peace
- Shield of faith
- Helmet of salvation
- Sword of the Spirit

In addition to wearing armor, the Christian is to face every occasion with prayer and to remember the fellow saints in prayer (v. 18).

Ultimately, however, the battle is not ours but God's (2 Chronicles 20:15). He knows the battle plan. Our responsibility is only to be active and obedient in the small duties, wherever he has placed us.

Charles Wesley, the writer of "Soldiers of Christ, Arise," knew much about the Christian life as warfare. Many times both Charles and his brother John were physically abused for their evangelical ministries. This hymn text was first published in 1749 and was titled "The Whole Armor of God—Ephesians VI." The hymn has often been referred to as "the Christian's bugle blast" for its strong call to battle.

LIVING THE MELODY

Whether you are in a time of struggle or rest, connect with your fellow believers. Reflect on how you and your fellow believers can encourage one another to put on the full armor of God.

What Scripture Says

Above all, you must live as citizens of heaven, conducting yourselves in a manner worthy of the Good News about Christ. Then, whether I come and see you again or only hear about you, I will know that you are standing together with one spirit and one purpose, fighting together for the faith, which is the Good News. Don't be intimidated in any way by your enemies. This will be a sign to them that they are going to be destroyed, but that you are going to be saved, even by God himself. For you have been given not only the privilege of trusting in Christ but also the privilege of suffering for him. We are in this struggle together.

—Philippians 1:27–30 NLT

Wisdom from History

You must never be afraid, if you are troubled by a flood of thoughts, that the enemy is too strong against you, that his attacks are never ending, that the war will last for your lifetime, and that you cannot avoid incessant downfalls of all kinds. Know that our enemies, with all their wiles, are in the hands of our divine Commander, our Lord Jesus Christ, for Whose honour and glory you are waging war. Since He himself leads you into battle, He will certainly not suffer your enemies to use violence against you and overcome you, if you do not yourself cross over to their side with your will.

He will Himself fight for you and will deliver your enemies
into your hands, when He wills and as He wills, as it is written: 'The Lord thy God walketh in the midst of thy camp,
to deliver thee, and to give up thine enemies before thee'
(Deut. xxiii. 14).[31]
—Lorenzo Scupoli (ca. 1530–1610)

Scupoli was unjustly accused of breaking the rules of his order
and stripped of his authority and all privileges. He was completely
exonerated, but not until a few years before his death. However,
he did not allow the shame to stop him. He wrote a widely published practical spiritual manual for living called *The Combat*, which
teaches trusting in God's power, not our own.

Application Questions
- Which piece of the armor of God do you struggle to put on?
  Why?
- What can you do today to strengthen that area of your spiritual
  walk?
- Can you ask someone in your life to help you grow in that area?

SAVIOR, LIKE A SHEPHERD LEAD US

1. Sav - ior, like a shep-herd lead us: Much we need Thy ten-d'rest care;
2. We are Thine; do Thou be - friend us; Be the Guard-ian of our way;
3. Thou hast prom-ised to re - ceive us, Poor and sin - ful tho' we be;
4. Ear - ly let us seek Thy fa - vor, Ear - ly let us do Thy will;

In Thy pleas - ant pas-tures feed us, For our use Thy folds pre - pare:
Keep Thy flock, from sin de - fend us, Seek us when we go a - stray:
Thou hast mer - cy to re - lieve us, Grace to cleanse, and pow'r to free:
Bless - ed Lord and on - ly Sav - ior, With Thy love our bos - oms fill:

Bless - ed Je - sus, Bless - ed Je - sus, Thou hast bought us, Thine we are;
Bless - ed Je - sus, Bless - ed Je - sus, Hear, O hear us when we pray;
Bless - ed Je - sus, bless - ed Je - sus, Ear - ly let us turn to Thee;
Bless - ed Je - sus, Bless - ed Je - sus, Thou hast loved us, love us still;

Bless-ed Je - sus, Bless - ed Je - sus, Thou hast bought us, Thine we are.
Bless-ed Je - sus, Bless - ed Je - sus, Hear, O hear us when we pray.
Bless-ed Je - sus, bless - ed Je - sus, Ear - ly let us turn to Thee.
Bless-ed Je - sus, Bless - ed Je - sus, Thou hast loved us, love us still.

Words: Dorothy A. Thrupp
Music: William B. Bradbury

— 26 —
SAVIOR, LIKE A SHEPHERD LEAD US

I will instruct you and teach you
in the way you should go;
I will counsel you with my loving eye on you.
—Psalm 32:8

DIVINE GUIDANCE IS THE VERY essence of Christianity. The Bible equates being guided by the Spirit of God with being a child of God (Romans 8:14). But even as children can sometimes rebel against parental authority, so too can we forsake God's leading in our lives and seek to go our own ways.

God's leading, then, doesn't just happen. We must have a sincere desire and willingness to be guided. With implicit faith, we must recognize that God has a planned path for his children, and we must deeply desire to follow that path wherever it leads. Scriptural promises such as Jeremiah 29:11 become our source of daily encouragement: "'I know the plans I have for you,' declares the LORD, 'plans to prosper you and not to harm you, plans to give you hope and a future.'"

The likely author of "Savior, Like a Shepherd Lead Us," Dorothy A. Thrupp, was born and lived in London, England. She was a prolific writer of children's hymns and devotional materials, although she seldom signed her name to any of her works. When she did, she used a pseudonym. For this reason it has never been fully proven that Thrupp was the actual author of this popular hymn. The hymn first appeared unsigned in her collection *Hymns for the Young* in 1836.

LIVING THE MELODY

Notice that both Scripture and the hymn "Savior, Like a Shepherd Lead Us" use language of community. In Jeremiah 29:11, "you" refers collectively to the entire nation of Israel, and the hymn calls "us" to turn to God and ask for guidance. It is as if we have an individual path to take that God has woven with the journeys of other believers to create his perfect plan.

Today, come together with your fellow believers and ask for God's guidance. Then walk your individual path one step at a time in the confidence of God's leading and presence.

What Scripture Says

We can make our own plans,
   but the LORD gives the right answer.

People may be pure in their own eyes,
   but the LORD examines their motives.

Commit your actions to the LORD,
   and your plans will succeed. . . .

We can make our plans,
   but the LORD determines our steps.
                    —Proverbs 16:1–3, 9 NLT

Wisdom from History

Lord, I am no longer my own, but Yours. Put me to what You will, rank me with whom You will. Let be employed by You or laid aside for You, exalted for You or brought low by You. Let me have all things, let me have nothing, I freely and heartily yield all things to Your pleasure and disposal. And now, O glorious and blessed God, Father, Son, and Holy Spirit, You are mine and I am Yours. So be it. Amen.[32]

                    —John Wesley (1703–1791)

Wesley was an English theologian who traveled throughout Great Britain and Ireland preaching about Christ and helping develop small groups with the purpose of fostering discipleship through religious instruction. His work contributed to the evangelical revival that occured in Britain, and the world, in the mid-eighteenth century.

Application Questions

- In what area of your life do you need guidance?
- How can your community help you discover God's path?
- Can you share your need with others?

WHO IS ON THE LORD'S SIDE?

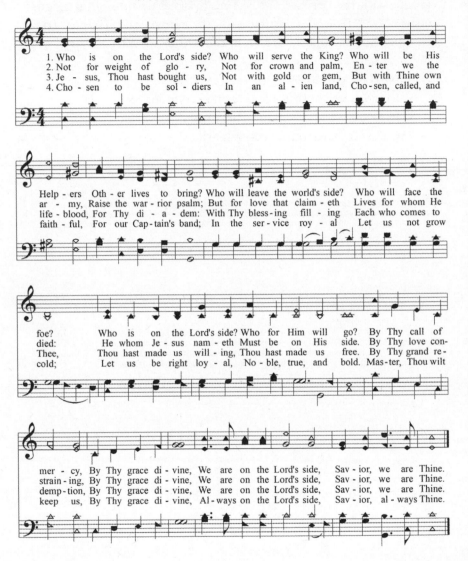

1. Who is on the Lord's side? Who will serve the King? Who will be His
2. Not for weight of glo - ry, Not for crown and palm, En - ter we the
3. Je - sus, Thou hast bought us, Not with gold or gem, But with Thine own
4. Cho - sen to be sol - diers In an al - ien land, Cho - sen, called, and

Help - ers Oth - er lives to bring? Who will leave the world's side? Who will face the
ar - my, Raise the war - rior psalm; But for love that claim - eth Lives for whom He
life - blood, For Thy di - a - dem: With Thy bless - ing fill - ing Each who comes to
faith - ful, For our Cap - tain's band; In the ser - vice roy - al Let us not grow

foe? Who is on the Lord's side? Who for Him will go? By Thy call of
died: He whom Je - sus nam - eth Must be on His side. By Thy love con-
Thee, Thou hast made us will - ing, Thou hast made us free. By Thy grand re-
cold; Let us be right loy - al, No - ble, true, and bold. Mas - ter, Thou wilt

mer - cy, By Thy grace di - vine, We are on the Lord's side, Sav - ior, we are Thine.
strain - ing, By Thy grace di - vine, We are on the Lord's side, Sav - ior, we are Thine.
demp - tion, By Thy grace di - vine, We are on the Lord's side, Sav - ior, we are Thine.
keep us, By Thy grace di - vine, Al - ways on the Lord's side, Sav - ior, al - ways Thine.

Words: Frances R. Havergal
Music: Sir John Goss

PDHymns.com

WHO IS ON THE LORD'S SIDE?

*Offer yourselves to God as those who have been
brought from death to life; and offer every part of
yourself to him as an instrument of righteousness.*
—Romans 6:13

AS CHRISTIANS, WE ARE TO take our places in God's spiritual army and not be ashamed to be counted as one of his. Believers are too often content to sit on the sidelines and merely observe. But the work of the gospel, inviting individuals to be personally reconciled with God, is an urgent task, not a spectator sport. It demands our whole-hearted, zealous involvement.

The text for this militant hymn, "Who Is on the Lord's Side?" by Frances R. Havergal, was originally titled "Home Missions" and was written in October 1877. It was based on the Scripture setting in 1 Chronicles 12:1–18, where a select group of soldiers was preparing to join David in warfare against the enemy. The poem later appeared in *Loyal Responses*, published by the author in 1878.

"Who Is on the Lord's Side?" has been used for more than a century to challenge Christians to make a definite commitment to follow Christ into spiritual warfare.

LIVING THE MELODY

Think about the people in your life who are not believers. Pray for opportunities to show, through your actions and words, the love and freedom that can only be found in Christ.

If you have been sitting on the sidelines, ask God to increase your zeal. Determine to join the battle, "not against flesh and blood, but against the rulers, against the authorities, against the powers of this dark world and against the spiritual forces of evil in the heavenly realms" (Ephesians 6:12).

What Scripture Says

If serving the LORD seems undesirable to you, then choose for yourselves this day whom you will serve, whether the gods your ancestors served beyond the Euphrates, or the gods of the Amorites, in whose land you are living. But as for me and my household, we will serve the LORD.

—Joshua 24:15

[Jesus] called the crowd to him along with his disciples and said: "Whoever wants to be my disciple must deny themselves and take up their cross and follow me. For whoever wants to save their life will lose it, but whoever loses their life for me and for the gospel will save it. What good is it for someone to gain the whole world, yet forfeit their soul? Or what can anyone give in exchange for their soul? If anyone is ashamed of me and my words in this adulterous and sinful generation, the Son of Man will be ashamed of them when he comes in his Father's glory with the holy angels."

—Mark 8:34–38

Wisdom from History

People are unreasonable, illogical, and self-centered. Love them anyway. If you are kind, people may accuse you of selfish ulterior motives. Be kind anyway. If you are successful, you will win some false friends and true enemies. Succeed anyway. The good you do today will be forgotten tomorrow. Be good anyway. Honesty and frankness will make you vulnerable. Be honest and frank anyway. What you spend years building may be destroyed overnight. Build anyway. People need help but may attack you if you try to help them. Help them anyway. In the final analysis, it is between you and God. It was never between you and them anyway.[33]

—Mother Teresa (1910–1997)

Mother Teresa was an Albanian-Indian nun who dedicated her life to helping the poor and outcast. She founded Missionaries of Charity, a congregation that not only runs soup kitchens, mobile medical clinics, orphanages, and schools, but also manages homes for people dying of HIV/AIDS, leprosy, and tuberculosis.

Application Questions
- What is one thing you can do today to serve the Lord?
- What are some things that typically hold you back from reaching out to help those around you?

WHAT A FRIEND WE HAVE IN JESUS

CONVERSE

Joseph Scriven, 1819-1886

Charles C. Converse, 1832-1918

1. What a Friend we have in Je - sus, All our sins and griefs to bear!
2. Have we tri - als and temp-ta - tions? Is there trou-ble an - y - where?
3. Are we weak and heav-y - la - den, Cum-bered with a load of care?

What a priv-i - lege to car - ry Ev - 'ry-thing to God in prayer!
We should nev-er be dis - cour-aged— Take it to the Lord in prayer.
Pre - cious Sav-ior, still our ref - uge— Take it to the Lord in prayer.

O what peace we oft - en for - feit, O what need-less pain we bear,
Can we find a friend so faith- ful Who will all our sor-rows share?
Do thy friends de-spise, for - sake thee? Take it to the Lord in prayer;

All be-cause we do not car - ry Ev - 'ry-thing to God in prayer!
Je - sus knows our ev-'ry weak-ness— Take it to the Lord in prayer.
In His arms He'll take and shield thee— Thou wilt find a sol - ace there.

– 28 –
WHAT A FRIEND WE HAVE IN JESUS

A man who has friends must himself be friendly,
But there is a friend who sticks closer than a brother.
—Proverbs 18:24 NKJV

A TRUE FRIEND LOVES AND accepts us just as we are, stays close to us in good or in bad, and is always ready to help in time of need. Because the author of "What a Friend We Have in Jesus" found just such a friend in his Lord, he decided to spend his entire life showing real friendship to others.

Joseph Scriven was born in 1819 in Dublin, Ireland. He had wealth, education, a devoted family, and a pleasant life. Then unexpected tragedy entered. On the night before Scriven's wedding, his fiancée drowned. In his deep sorrow, Joseph realized he could find the solace and support he needed only in his dearest friend, Jesus.

Soon after this tragedy, Scriven dramatically changed his lifestyle. He left Ireland for Port Hope, Canada, determined to devote all his extra time to being a friend and helper to others. He took the Sermon on the Mount seriously, often giving away his clothing and possessions to those in need.

A man once saw Scriven carrying his saw through town and asked, "Who is that man? I want him to work for me." The answer was, "You cannot get that man; he saws wood only for poor widows and sick people who cannot pay." Scriven became known as "the Good Samaritan of Port Hope."

When Scriven's mother became ill in Ireland, he wrote a comforting letter to her, enclosing the words of his newly written poem with the prayer that the brief lines would remind her of a never-failing heavenly Friend. Sometime later, when Joseph Scriven himself was ill, a friend who came to call on him happened to see a copy of these words scribbled on scratch paper near his bed. The friend read the lines with interest and asked, "Who wrote those beautiful words?"

"The Lord and I did it between us" was Scriven's reply.[34]

LIVING THE MELODY

While we are created to be in human community, the reality is that Jesus is the only one who can fully bear all our sins and griefs. In him we have one true place of refuge, one true person who knows our every weakness, one true friend who will lift our burden . . . if we take it to the Lord in prayer.

Take a few quiet minutes to process where you're hurting and needing the support only Jesus can give. Then pray for the Lord's care. Like Joseph Scriven, we too can find relief from our burdens when we turn to our Lord as a friend. Out of this foundational friendship, we can then offer genuine friendship to others.

What Scripture Says

The LORD has heard my cry for mercy;
  the LORD accepts my prayer.
                              —Psalm 6:9

We are confident that he hears us whenever we ask for anything that pleases him. And since we know he hears us when we make our requests, we also know that he will give us what we ask for.
                              —1 John 5:14–15 NLT

Wisdom from History

Whenever God begins something, we have the assurance that He will finish it. Nothing will stand in the way of Him accomplishing His purpose in this world and in our lives. What God starts, He finishes, and nobody can hinder Him.

Sure, delays will happen. Just remember, God is in charge of the delays as well as the progress.[35]

—A. W. Tozer (1897–1963)

Tozer was a pastor and author known for his total devotion to God through prayer and the study of his Word.

Application Questions

- Where are you feeling burdened and hurting?
- What steps can you take to move your burden to Christ?

WHEN WE ALL GET TO HEAVEN

1. Sing the won-drous love of Je - sus, Sing His mer - cy and His grace:
2. While we walk the pil - grim path-way, Clouds will o - ver - spread the sky;
3. Let us then be true and faith-ful, Trust - ing, serv - ing ev - 'ry day;

In the man - sions bright and bless - ed, He'll pre - pare for us a place.
But when trav - 'ling days are o - ver, Not a shad-ow, not a sigh.
Just one glimpse of Him in glo - ry Will the toils of life re - pay.
(1. He'll pre - pare for us a place.)

Chorus

When we all get to heav - en, What a day of re - joic - ing
When we all What a day

that will be! When we all see Je - sus,
of re - joic - ing that will be! When we all

We'll sing and shout the vic - to - ry.
and shout the vic - to - ry.

Words: E. E. Hewitt
Music: Mrs. J. G. Wilson

WHEN WE ALL GET TO HEAVEN

After that, we who are still alive and are left
will be caught up together with them in the clouds
to meet the Lord in the air. And so we will be
with the Lord forever. Therefore encourage
each other with these words.
—1 Thessalonians 4:17–18

FOR THE CHILD OF GOD, the end of this earthly pilgrimage is just the beginning of a glorious new life.

Our services of worship should be a foretaste of that day of rejoicing when those from every tribe, language, people, and nation see our Lord and together "sing and shout the victory."

The author of this hymn text, Eliza E. Hewitt, a schoolteacher in Philadelphia, was a Christian lay worker deeply devoted to the Sunday school movement during the latter half of the nineteenth century.

Like many of the other gospel songwriters of that time, Hewitt wrote her lyrics with the goal of teaching children the truths of the gospel. She often attended the Methodist camp meetings at Ocean Grove, New Jersey. It was there that she collaborated with Emily Wilson, wife of a district superintendent in Philadelphia, in the writing of this popular gospel hymn, a favorite of both young and old. It was first published in 1898.

The anticipation of heaven has often been described as the oxygen of the human soul. "All who have this hope in him purify themselves, just as he is pure" (1 John 3:3).

LIVING THE MELODY

Allow yourself to imagine with anticipation that day in heaven when the entire family of God is gathered for an endless celebration of praise. May this glorious hope brighten your day, unite you with other believers, and keep you "true and faithful, trusting, serving."

What Scripture Says

You will show me the way of life,
   granting me the joy of your presence
   and the pleasures of living with you forever.
                              —Psalm 16:11 NLT

Those who have been ransomed by the LORD will return.
   They will enter Jerusalem singing,
   crowned with everlasting joy.
Sorrow and mourning will disappear,
   and they will be filled with joy and gladness.
                              —Isaiah 35:10 NLT

My Father's house has many rooms; if that were not so, would I have told you that I am going there to prepare a place for you? And if I go and prepare a place for you, I will come back and take you to be with me that you also may be where I am.
                              —John 14:2–3

Wisdom from History

O my dear parishioners, let us endeavor to get to heaven! There we shall see God. How happy we shall feel! If the parish is converted we shall go there in procession with the parish priest at the head. . . . We must get to heaven![36]
                              —Saint John Vianney (1786–1859)

Saint John Vianney is the patron saint of parish priests. He was designated as such due to the way he focused on reestablishing spiritual knowledge in his local parish after the French Revolution.

Application Questions

- What is one aspect of heaven you're looking forward to?
- How does thinking about heaven help you in the here and now?

GOD BE WITH YOU

Jeremiah E. Rankin, 1828-1904

William G. Tomer, 1833-1896

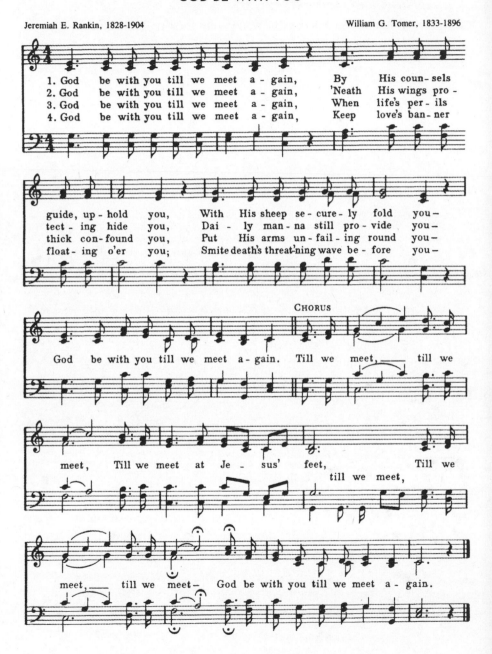

1. God be with you till we meet a - gain, By His coun - sels
2. God be with you till we meet a - gain, 'Neath His wings pro -
3. God be with you till we meet a - gain, When life's per - ils
4. God be with you till we meet a - gain, Keep love's ban - ner

guide, up - hold you, With His sheep se - cure - ly fold you —
tect - ing hide you, Dai - ly man - na still pro - vide you —
thick con - found you, Put His arms un - fail - ing round you —
float - ing o'er you; Smite death's threat'ning wave be - fore you —

CHORUS

God be with you till we meet a - gain. Till we meet, till we

meet, Till we meet at Je - sus' feet, Till we
till we meet,

meet, till we meet — God be with you till we meet a - gain.

— 30 —

GOD BE WITH YOU

The LORD bless you
and keep you;
the LORD make his face shine on you
and be gracious to you;
the LORD turn his face toward you
and give you peace.
—Numbers 6:24–26

OFTEN WE HEAR SOMEONE TELL us glibly to "have a good day!" Would not a far better farewell for Christians be the loving wish of today's hymn text, "God be with you"? The added thought of "till we meet again" suggests a sincere desire for continued friendship.

The writer of "God Be with You," Jeremiah E. Rankin, pastored several prominent Congregational churches throughout the East until 1889, when he became president of Howard University.

A powerful preacher and an excellent leader and promoter of congregational singing, Rankin wrote much poetry, including the still-popular hymn "Tell It to Jesus." He also edited several well-known gospel songbooks.

No other hymn, except perhaps "Blest Be the Tie That Binds," has been as widely used as "God Be with You" for a closing benediction in church services. It was a favorite in the Moody-Sankey meetings throughout North America and England. It was the official closing song for the Christian Endeavor conventions around the world. And still today, no finer farewell can be expressed by Christians to one another as they leave a place of worship than the sincere wish, "God be with you till we meet again."

LIVING THE MELODY

Words are powerful. Challenge yourself this week to avoid trite and casual greetings and farewells. Instead, practice a genuine, God-given concern for your community. Try saying goodbye to friends or family with some of the lovely wishes expressed in this hymn: God be with you . . . guide and uphold you, hide you, put his arms around you.

What Scripture Says

Now I commit you to God and to the word of his grace, which can build you up and give you an inheritance among all those who are sanctified.

—Acts 20:32

And the God of all grace, who called you to his eternal glory in Christ, after you have suffered a little while, will himself restore you and make you strong, firm and steadfast.

—1 Peter 5:10

Wisdom from History

It is my joy in life to find
At every turning of the road,
The strong arm of a comrade kind
To help me onward with my load.
And since I have no gold to give,
And love alone can make amends,
My daily prayer is, while I live,—
God, make me worthy of my friends![37]
—Frank D. Sherman (1860–1916)

Sherman was an American poet, architect, and mathematician. He graduated from Columbia College and taught there for much of his career.

Application Questions

- Think of a time when you were bolstered by your community. What things did your community say or do to support you?
- In what other ways can you remind fellow believers that God will never leave them?

NOTES

1. Dave and Jon Ferguson, *B.L.E.S.S.: 5 Everyday Ways to Love Your Neighbor and Change the World* (Washington, DC: Salem Books, 2021).
2. *The Little Flowers of St. Francis*, trans. James Rhoades (New York: E. P. Dutton, 1904), 86, www.google.com/books/edi tion/The_Little_Flowers_of_St_Francis_of_Assi/qWEaAAA AMAAJ?hl=en&gbpv=1.
3. Dorothy Day, *The Long Loneliness*, quoted in "Richard Foster—Evangelical Sparkplug," January 8, 2015, www.wayoflife .org/database/richardfoster.html.
4. *Mere Christianity*, in *The Complete C. S. Lewis Signature Classics* (United Kingdom: HarperCollins, 2007), 159.
5. Richard J. Foster and James Bryan Smith, eds., *Devotional Classics: Selected Readings for Individuals and Groups*, rev. ed. (New York: HarperCollins, 2005), 261.
6. Foster and Smith, *Devotional Classics*, 318–19.
7. Evelyn Underhill, *Worship* (Eugene, OR: Wipf and Stock, 2002), 18.
8. Benedicta Ward, trans., *The Sayings of the Desert Fathers: The Alphabetical Collection*, rev. ed. (Trappist, KY: Cistercian, 1984), s.vv. "Anthony the Great, 3."
9. Thomas à Kempis, *The Imitation of Christ*, trans. Aloysius Croft and Harold Bolton (Mineola, NY: Dover, 2003), 35.
10. "The Purpose of Church Hymns by St Theophan the Recluse," in "10 Passages About Music and Its Effect on the Spiritual Life," February 22, 2019, *The Art of Orthodoxy* (blog), https:// theartoforthodoxy.com/2019/02/22/quotes-on-music.

11. J. I. Packer, *Knowing God* (Downers Grove, IL: InterVarsity, 1973), 23.
12. John Greenleaf Whittier, quoted in John Julian, *A Dictionary of Hymnology* (Grand Rapids: Kregel, 1985), 1278.
13. "Sayings & Stories of the Desert Fathers," Monastery of Christ in the Desert, accessed September 10, 2023, https://christdesert .org/prayer/desert-fathers-stories/on-humility/#:—:text=He %20also%20said%2C%20"If%20when,they%20are%20accept able%20to%20God.
14. Samuel Rutherford, *The Trial and Triumph of Faith* (Edinburgh: General Assembly of the Free Church of Scotland, 1845), 99.
15. Ignatius of Loyola, "The First Principle and Foundation," in "Prayers of Ignatius of Loyola," Presbyterian Church (USA), accessed September 11, 2023, www.pcusa.org/site_media/me dia/uploads/oga/pdf/prayers-of-ignatius-of-loyola.pdf.
16. Ward, *The Sayings of the Desert Fathers*, s.vv. "Orsisius, 1."
17. Ernest Edwin Ryden, *The Story of Our Hymns* (Rock Island, IL: Augustana Book Concern, 1931), 312.
18. Amy Carmichael, *Edges of His Ways: Daily Devotional Notes* (Fort Washington, PA: CLC Publications, 2011), 175–76.
19. Susanna Wesley, in a letter to John Wesley, June 8, 1725, "What Is a Sin?," Resources: Christian Missions and World Evangelism (website), accessed September 12, 2023, home.snu.edu/~hculbert /sin.htm.
20. Henry Mason Baum, ed., *The American Church Review* 41, no. 5 (May 1883): 500.
21. Suzanne Noffke, *Catherine of Siena: An Anthology* (Tempe, AZ: ACMRS Press, 2011), 395.
22. Ward, *The Sayings of the Desert Fathers*, s.vv. "Nisterus, 2."
23. Basil the Great, *The Treatise De Spiritu Sancto*, IX, 23.
24. Athanasius, *On the Incarnation of the Word*, quoted in William A. Dembski, Wayne J. Downs, and Fr. Justin G. A. Frederick, eds., *The Patristic Understanding of Creation: An Anthology*

of Writings from the Church Fathers on Creation and Design (Nashville: Erasmus Press, 2008), ch. XLIII.

25. Emily May Grimes, "The Quiet Hour," 1920, public domain.

26. Henri J. M. Nouwen, *A Cry for Mercy: Prayers from the Genesee* (New York: Image, 2002), 35.

27. "Status of Global Christianity, 2024, in the Context of 1900–2050," https://static1.squarespace.com/static/4f661fde24ac 1097e013deea/t/65bd27b23fbd8e4b9cf7e1d0/17068952 82534/Status-of-Global-Christianity-2024.pdf, derived from Gina A., Zurlo, Todd M. Johnson, and Peter F. Crossing, "World Christianity 2024: Fragmentation and Unity," *International Bulletin of Mission Research* 49, no. 1 (January 2024): 43–45, https://doi.org/10.1177/23969393231201817.

28. "Global Dashboard," Joshua Project, accessed February 8, 2024, https://joshuaproject.net/people_groups/dashboard.

29. Foster and Smith, *Devotional Classics*, 324–25.

30. "Lorica of St. Patrick," Catholic Online, accessed September 18, 2023, www.catholic.org/prayers/prayer.php?p=302.

31. Lorenzo Scupoli, *Unseen Warfare: The Spiritual Combat and Path to Paradise of Lorenzo Scupoli*, ed. Nicodemus of the Holy Mountain, rev. Theophan the Recluse, trans. E. Kadloubovsky and G. E. H. Palmer (Crestwood, NY: St. Vladimir's Seminary Press, 1987), 111.

32. *John and Charles Wesley: Selected Prayers, Hymns, Journal Notes, Sermons, Letters and Treatises*, ed. Frank Whaling (Mahwah, NJ: Paulist Press, 1981), 387.

33. Jim Palmer, comp., *Big Wisdom (Little Book): 1,001 Proverbs, Adages, and Precepts to Help You Live a Better Life* (Nashville: Thomas Nelson, 2005), 88. This quote was on a sign on the wall of a children's home in Calcutta. It is typically attributed to Mother Teresa.

34. Robert J. Morgan, *Then Sings My Soul: 150 of the World's Greatest Hymn Stories* (Nashville: Thomas Nelson, 2022), 131.

35. A. W. Tozer, *My Daily Pursuit: Devotions for Every Day* (Grand Rapids: Baker, 2013), 329.
36. René Fourrey, *The Curé D'Ars: A Pictorial Biography*, trans. Ruth Mary Bethel (United Kingdom: P. J. Kenedy & Sons, 1960), 133.
37. Frank Dempster Sherman, "A Prayer," in *Lyrics of Joy* (Boston: Houghton, Mifflin, 1904), 30.

SELECTED BIBLIOGRAPHY

Bailey, Albert B. *The Gospel in Hymns*. New York: Charles Scribner's Sons, 1950.

Barrows, Cliff, ed. *Crusade Hymn Stories*. Chicago: Hope Publishing, 1967.

Benson, Louis F. *The English Hymn*. New York: George H. Doran, 1915. Reprint, Louisville: John Knox, 1962.

Blanchard, Kathleen. *Stories of Favorite Hymns*. Grand Rapids: Zondervan, 1940.

Brown, Theron, and Hezekiah Butterworth. *The Story of the Hymns and Tunes*. New York: George H. Doran, 1906.

Clark, W. Thorburn. *Stories of Fadeless Hymns*. Nashville: Broadman, 1949.

Davies, James P. *Sing with Understanding*. Chicago: Covenant, 1966.

Douglas, Charles W. *Church Music in History and Practice*. New York: Charles Scribner's Sons, 1937. Revised 1962 by Leonard Ellinwood.

Emurian, Ernest K. *Living Stories of Famous Hymns*. Boston: W. A. Wilde, 1955.

Erickson, J. Irving. *Twice-Born Hymns*. Chicago: Covenant, 1976.

Frost, Maurice. *Historical Companion to Hymns Ancient and Modern*. London: William Clowes and Sons, 1962.

Gabriel, C. H. *The Singers and Their Songs*. Winona Lake, IN: Rodeheaver, 1915.

Hagedorn, Ivan H. *Stories of Great Hymn Writers*. Grand Rapids: Zondervan, 1948.

Hustad, Donald P. *Hymns for the Living Church*. Carol Stream, IL: Hope Publishing, 1978.

————. *Dictionary-Handbook to Hymns for the Living Church.* Carol Stream, IL: Hope Publishing.

————. *Jubilate! Church Music in the Evangelical Tradition.* Carol Stream, IL: Hope Publishing.

Julian, John. *A Dictionary of Hymnology.* 2 volumes. New York: Charles Scribner's Sons, 1892. Reprint, Grand Rapids: Kregel, 1985.

Kerr, Phil. *Music in Evangelism and Stories of Famous Christian Songs.* Glendale, CA: Gospel Music Publishers, 1939.

Lillenas, Haldor. *Modern Gospel Song Stories.* Kansas City, MO: Lillenas, 1952.

Loewen, Alice, Harold Moyer, and Mary Oyer. *Exploring the Mennonite Hymnal: Handbook.* Newton, KS: Faith and Life, 1983.

Marks, Harvey B. *The Rise and Growth of English Hymnody.* New York: Fleming H. Revell, 1938.

McCutchan, Robert G. *Hymn Tune Names, Their Sources and Significance.* New York: Abingdon, 1957.

————. *Our Hymnody: A Manual of the Methodist Hymnal.* 2nd ed. New York and Nashville: Abingdon-Cokesbury, 1942.

Peterson, John W. *The Miracle Goes On.* Grand Rapids: Zondervan, 1976.

Reynolds, William J., and Milburn Price. *A Joyful Sound: Christian Hymnody.* New York: Holt, Rinehart and Winston, 1978.

Reynolds, William J. *Hymns of Our Faith, A Handbook for the Baptist Hymnal.* Nashville: Broadman, 1964.

————. *Companion to the Baptist Hymnal.* Nashville: Broadman, 1976.

Routley, Erik. *Hymns Today and Tomorrow.* New York: Abingdon, 1964.

————. *Hymns and the Faith.* Grand Rapids: Eerdmans, 1968.

Rudin, Cecilia Margaret. *Stories of Hymns We Love.* Chicago: John Rudin, 1945.

Ruffin, Bernard. *Fanny Crosby.* New York: United Church Press, 1976.

Ryden, Ernest Edwin. *The Story of Christian Hymnody.* Rock Island, IL: Augustana Press, 1959.

Sallee, James. *A History of Evangelistic Hymnody.* Grand Rapids: Baker Book House, 1978.

Sankey, Ira D. *My Life and the Story of the Gospel Hymns.* New York: Harper and Brothers, 1906.

Sanville, George W. *Forty Gospel Hymn Stories.* Winona Lake, IN: Rodeheaver-Hall-Mack, 1943.

Sellers, E. O. *Evangelism in Sermon and Song.* Chicago: Moody Press, 1946.

Shea, George Beverly. *Songs That Lift the Heart.* With Fred Bauer. New York: Fleming H. Revell, 1972.

Smith, Oswald J. *Oswald J. Smith's Hymn Stories.* Winona Lake, IN: Rodeheaver, 1963.

Stebbins, George C. *Reminiscences and Gospel Hymn Stories.* New York: George H. Doran, 1924.

Sydnor, James R. *The Hymn and Congregational Singing.* Richmond, VA: John Knox, 1960.

Thompson, Ronald W. *Who's Who of Hymn Writers.* London: Epworth, 1967.

Wake, Arthur N. *Companion to Hymnbook for Christian Worship.* St. Louis, MO: Bethany Press, 1970.

ABOUT THE AUTHOR

Kenneth W. Osbeck (MA, University of Michigan) taught for thirty-five years, first at Grand Rapids School of the Bible and Music and then at Grand Rapids Baptist College and Seminary. He also served as music director for Children's Bible Hour, Radio Bible Class, and many churches. He authored several books, including the best-selling *Amazing Grace: 366 Inspiring Hymn Stories for Daily Devotions*; *101 Hymn Stories: The Inspiring True Stories Behind 101 Favorite Hymns*; *101 More Hymn Stories: The Inspiring True Stories Behind 101 Favorite Hymns*; and *Devotional Warm-Ups for the Church Choir: Preparing to Lead Others in Worship*.

ABOUT THE EDITOR

Janyre Tromp is an award-winning and best-selling author with a deep love for history. Her books include *Shadows in the Mind's Eye*, *O Little Town*, and *Darkness Calls the Tiger*. Find her on social media or her website, janyretromp.com.